2ND EDITION

EXECUTIVE FUNCTIONING Workbook

PUTTING THE PUZZLE PIECES TOGETHER:

- EXECUTIVE FUNCTIONING
- SOCIAL EMOTIONAL SKILLS
- SELF-REGULATION

NEW! INSTRUCTOR GUIDE INCLUDED

2nd Edition

About the Authors

Karen Fried and Melissa Mullin founded the K&M Center, an educational institution dedicated to transforming the lives of neurodivergent children and adolescents. Their innovative approach combined personalized, evidence-based strategies and a deep understanding of individual learning profiles to help students unlock their full potential. Now consultants to those serving neurodiverse students, they have written the 2nd edition of their book on *Executive Functioning: Executive Functioning Workbook: Putting the Puzzle Pieces Together*. This book teaches the fundamental skills of executive functioning using a holistic and experiential approach.

Other publications by Karen Fried and Melissa Mullin: *The Adult Executive Functioning Workbook, A Maze the Brain, Flexible Thinking Program, Think, Talk, Laugh* and *By The Rules: One Syllable Spelling*.

Karen Fried, Psy.D., M.F.T. is a licensed Marriage and Family Therapist and an Educational Therapist and consultant in Santa Monica, California. She has a private practice in Psychotherapy. Karen uses the Oaklander Model of Child Therapy in her practice and is the President of the Violet Solomon Oaklander Foundation. Karen's integration of Gestalt Play Therapy using Oaklander Model while also supporting neurodiverse students at the K&M Center provided a holistic and compassionate approach to supporting individuals with neurodiverse learning profiles. She trains child and adolescent therapists and educators in the US and internationally. Training, online tools, and many resources can be found at oaklandertraining.org. Karen can be reached at karen@karenfried.com.

Dr. Melissa Mullin's extensive background in educational psychology, combined with her dedication to supporting students and families, makes her a valuable resource in the field. Her journey, from her work at The Walt Disney Educational Media Company to earning a Ph.D. in Educational Psychology at UCLA, reflects her passion for education and learning. Her work as an Educational Consultant helps empower students to thrive in their educational pursuits by providing comprehensive assessments, personalized recommendations, and guidance to those involved in their education. Her dedication to helping families is evident in her blog, www.bitsofwisdomforall.com, where she shares valuable insights about academic learning and life skills. Melissa can be reached at Melissamullin.com

ISBN: 9798218910136
©2023 K&M Center, Inc. 3435 Ocean Park Blvd Santa Monica, CA 90405

Table of Contents

INTRODUCTION 9
Reimagining Executive Functioning 9
    Executive Functioning Skills 10
    Self-Regulation Skills 17
    Social-Emotional Skills 26
Key Concepts of this Program 26

INSTRUCTOR GUIDE 28
Teaching Executive Functioning Skills 28
Teaching Social-Emotional and Self-Regulation Skills 31
    Understanding and Using Oaklander Model Activities 31
        Your Role in Using the Oaklander Model 33
    The Process: Using the Oaklander Model to Strengthen EF 39
        The Treatment Plan: Blending Oaklander Model and EF Training 41
Preparing the Sessions 45
    Setting and Sharing Session Purpose and Process 45
    The Relationship 46
    Review: Points to Keep in Mind 50

STUDENT WORKBOOK 51
Goal of the Workbook 51
What is Executive Functioning? 51

How the Program Works 55

    The Flow of the Program 56

UNIT 1: EF QUESTIONNAIRE AND GOAL SETTING 58

Set Up a Successful Executive Functioning Plan 59

    Exercise: Your Executive Functioning Scores 60

    Student Interview 62

    Goal Setting 66

    Exercise: Write Your Goals 67

UNIT 2: STOP AND IMAGINE 70

Executive Functioning Skills that help you STOP AND IMAGINE 71

Inhibition: The ability to stop off-task actions when you need to 72

    Exercise: Clear Your Mind 74

Shifting: Moving from one idea or activity to another 75

    Exercise: Flex Your Brain 77

    Exercise: Inhibition with Stroop 78

    Exercise: Draw Infinity 79

    Exercise: How Many Ways 80

Emotional Control: Regulating stress and distractibility 81

    Exercise: Feeling Wheel 82

    Exercise: Feeling Pyramid 84

Monitoring: Judging the quality and pace of work 85

Organizing Materials: Organizing objects for work, play and storage 86

    Exercise: Rate Your Backpack and Workspace 87

Using your STOP AND IMAGINE skills 88
   Organize your Backpack 88
      Checklist: Morning Checklist 89
      Checklist: Afternoon Checklist 90
      Checklist: Quick Daily Backpack Checklist 91
      Checklist: Weekly Backpack Checklist 92
      Checklist: Backpack Organization 94
      Checklist: Nightly Sign Off 94
   Organize your Study Space 95
      Checklist: Workspace Needs 96
      Checklist: Workspace Materials Worksheet 97

UNIT 3: THINK AND PLAN: 100

Executive Functioning Skills that help you THINK AND PLAN: 101
   Working Memory: Remembering information for immediate use 102
      Exercise: Alphabet Memory Stretch 103
      Exercise: The Connection Game 104
   Shifting: Moving from one idea or activity to another 105
      Exercise: The Scribble Drawing 106
   Monitoring: Judging the quality and pace of work 108
      Exercise: Questions to Help You Monitor Your Progress 109
   Time Management: Allotting the correct amount of time for what you want to do 110
      Exercise: How Accurate is My Sense of Time 112
      Exercise: Internal Timekeepers 114
      Exercise: What Activities Fill Up Your Day? 116
      Exercise: Daily Schedule 117

    Exercise: Questions About Your Schedule 119

  Planning: Setting goals and the steps to accomplish them 120

    Exercise: Questions to Help You Plan 122

Using your THINK AND PLAN skills 123

  Using a Planner 123

    Exercise: Picking a Planner 123

    Checklist: How to Use a Planner 124

    Exercise: When to Use Your Planner 125

    Checklist: How to Use Your Planner 126

  Long-Term Planning 127

  Steps for Planning Essays, Projects, and Reports 128

    Checklist: Long-Term Planning 131

    Exercise: Monthly Calendar 132

  Calendar and Planner Apps 133

UNIT 4: DO AND REVIEW: 136

Executive Functioning skills that help you DO AND REVIEW 138

  Initiation: Starting Work 138

    Exercise: Turn the Procrastinator into the Initiator 140

  Emotional Control: Regulating stress and distractibility 142

    Exercise: Get Back on Task 143

    Exercise: The Feeling Wheel 144

    Exercise: The Gatekeeper 146

  Monitoring: Judging the quality and pace of your work 147

    Exercise: Daily Homework Planner 149

    Exercise: Nightly Homework Plan 152

Using your DO AND REVIEW Skills ... 157

Active Reading ... 157

Tools for Active Reading: ... 158

- Checklist: Character List 159
- Exercise: SQ3R (Survey, Question, Read, Recite, Review) ... 161
- Exercise: Chapter Summary ... 162
- Exercise: Active Reading Review ... 163
- Note-Taking Prompts ... 165
- Note-Taking Tips ... 166
- Format Notes ... 167
- Note-taking Apps ... 171

Studying for tests ... 173

- Steps to prepare for a presentation or exam ... 174
- Guiding Questions for a presentation or exam ... 175
- Steps to follow for true/false exams: ... 177
- Steps to follow for short-answer exams: ... 178
- Steps to follow for essay exams: ... 179
- Creating a Web to Help with Essay Responses: ... 180
- Steps to follow for math exams: ... 183

Apps to avoid distractions: ... 184

UNIT 5: CHECK AND TURN IN: ... 186

Executive Functioning skills that help you CHECK AND TURN IN ... 187

Monitoring: Judging the quality and pace of your work ... 188

- Exercise Self-Monitoring ... 189

Shifting: Moving from one idea or activity to another ... 190

Checklist: Is My Work Complete?...190

Inhibition: The ability to stop off task actions when you need to...........................191

Emotional Control: Regulating stress and distractibility......................................193

    Exercise: Who's in Charge?..194

    Exercise: Beginning, Middle, End..196

Using your CHECK AND TURN In skills...198

    Checklist: Guiding Questions to Check Your Work.................................198

    Checklist: Turn it in..199

UNIT 6: REASSESS..200

    Executive Functioning skills to review:..201

    Exercise: Rate Your Skills...202

    Exercise: Reflect On What Worked For You..204

    Plan for the future...204

APPENDIX..206

Introduction

Reimagining Executive Functioning

What do students need so they can plan and complete work effectively on their own? Short answer: **Executive Functioning**—the combined abilities to focus, follow instructions, organize thinking, and manage emotions and behavior to finish a task. Yet, these Executive Functioning (EF) capacities don't operate all alone. **Self-regulation** (awareness of one's thoughts and feelings, and control of one's actions) and **social-emotional** abilities (understanding and connecting to others) enable EF. In fact, these skill sets overlap and support each other. Self-regulation lets us set goals and curtail internal and external distractions from them; social-emotional sensitivity allows us to read others' cues and expectations and assess how well we're doing. In brief, for learners to use the executive functions of planning, starting, monitoring, adjusting, and completing work on their own, they also need self-regulation and social-emotional strengths. And since building EF skills requires a sense of self and a connection to others as well as organization and study strategies, this reimagined EF program helps students develop all those interdependent capacities.

The linkage of self-regulatory, social-emotional, and EF powers explains why children with learning differences or attentional weakness often struggle not only in class but in all venues (as do people of any age with poor EF). So, this program's *whole child* approach cultivates each equally important area of personal, social, and intellectual competence. While activities from various sources appear in the sessions, the program

Introduction

owes most to the theory and interventions of child and adolescent therapist Violet Oaklander, whose holistic, relational, "here-and-now" Gestalt Therapy orientation blazed a trail in work with youngsters. The Oaklander Model's engaging presence in these pages is the primary guide for our reimagined EF training.

For this reason, each workbook unit utilizes varied types of learning tools: creative, self-expressive, and connective exercises along with EF prompts and checklists. As Oaklander taught, open-ended, child-led activities bolster the sense of self and social-emotional abilities students need for self-regulation and interaction; at the same time, prompts and checklists provide structure for mastering specific EF skills. These interwoven tools reinforce each other to promote a student's learning independence.

This introduction will familiarize you with basic research, and clinical examples, on EF and the tools we use to strengthen it, especially those of the Oaklander Model. Then it will show you how the Student Workbook blends and expands each learner's EF, self-regulation, and social-emotional skills. (As a side note, that same respect for individuation and inclusivity led us to favor gender-neutral pronouns whenever possible in this text.)

Executive Functioning Skills

This umbrella term covers a range of capacities working together as the CEO of our brain. They let us look at a task, follow directions, identify and gather needed materials, estimate the time it will take, do the task, check it over, and turn it in. That process sounds obvious to anyone with strong EF abilities, yet it's extremely difficult for those without them. Fortunately, EF can be strengthened with guided effort. The first step on that journey? Pinpointing a person's weak skill or skills, and teaching strategies to cultivate them.

Components of EF: Definitions and Examples
- **Inhibition:** The ability to stop one's behavior at the appropriate time. For example, Jason always intends to do his homework promptly, but can't inhibit his tendency to instant-message friends or indulge in other distractions and ends up doing his assignments late at night when he's exhausted and panicked.
- **Shifting:** The ability to change from one activity to another with some flexibility. Kim, a high school student, never performed well if she had a substitute teacher. She also had difficulty generalizing a math concept she knew if the problem looked different from the one in her homework.
- **Initiation:** The capacity to start a task or return to it after a break. Kevin, a 12th-grader, would stare at his computer screen for up to 3 hours before finally beginning work on an essay.
- **Working Memory:** The ability to remember information for immediate use. For example, Working Memory enables learners to listen to class lectures and take good notes, perform basic mental math problems, and follow multi-step instructions. A parent described his son: "I told him to go up to his room, brush his teeth and put on his pajamas. Fifteen minutes later, I go up and he's getting his clothes out for the next day. But no pajamas, no brushed teeth."
- **Planning and Organizing:** The capability to manage current and future tasks by setting goals and identifying needed steps ahead of time, especially for long-term assignments and tests. For example, students who think there is "no homework" if a test is 4 days away most likely have difficulty planning and organizing.

Introduction

- **Organizing Materials and Time Management:** The ability to identify and gather appropriate materials and to budget necessary time for tasks. The state of a student's backpack speaks volumes: If it's neat and has everything required both for school and home, organizing materials is likely a strength. Many students, however, cannot organize their work and storage spaces, and therefore lack easy access to necessary supplies and, sometimes, even to their completed assignments. Similarly, many students battle the clock rather than manage their time, working too long or too hurriedly on tasks.

- **Monitoring:** The ability to judge the quality of one's work based on expected standards. Erin, a middle-school student, was the first to finish her Spanish quiz, happily turned it into the teacher, and later told her parents she thought she had done great on it. Her grade? The lowest in the class. Erin has difficulty assessing her performance as the teacher would. Students like Erin often have skewed perceptions of their efforts, do too much or too little, and do not catch their errors.

- **Emotional Control:** Regulating one's responses to stress in school or in life. Emotionally resilient students rebound quickly after a disappointing performance and persevere in their efforts, but those lacking emotional control do not. When Sara received what she thought was an unfair grade, she became angry and stopped working in class. Maggie, on the other hand, reacted to doing poorly on tests by staying up later and later to study 'just a little more." These girls show contrasting, but equally ineffective, responses to stress.

How Executive Functioning Skills Develop

EF skills emerge as early as preschool when children play nicely with others (emotional control) and move from one activity to the next (shifting). An early fostering of EF helps children organize not just their schoolwork but their thoughts and behavior.

Encouraging them to figure out puzzles sharpens their planning and problem-solving strengths. Constructing with blocks, exploring mazes, and imagining with choose-your-own-adventure books implant the cause-and-effect concept basic to science and other disciplines. Helping children check their own work to find and fix mistakes teaches self-monitoring and the sense of themselves as competent learners.

Younger students may exhibit few signs of EF difficulties because parents and teachers still manage much of their academic and social life. Yet as they grow, so do the expectations. In elementary and middle school, EF challenges may appear with increasing demands for socialization and independent problem-solving: They need to sit still longer, manage their emotions in more complex situations, listen to more information, and organize a heavier workload.

EF skills, then, develop as the life skills they are. Having strong EF lets youngsters know what they need or want to do, figure out the steps to do it, follow through on that plan, and finally determine how well the plan worked. No surprise, then, how significant a role EF capacities play in students' education.

The Increasing Impact of EF on Academic Areas
Elementary-school students learn the basics of reading comprehension, written language, and independent studying, homework, long-term project completion and test preparation. But by middle school these fundamental knacks must be wholly automatic so learners can integrate higher-order skills (like critique and generalizing) to a harder curriculum that carries greater expectations of self-agency and planning. Jennifer, an 8th grader, hates to write essays. While brilliant in discussions, her in-class

Introduction

and at-home writing assignments are brief and disorganized. Not surprisingly, Jennifer has difficulty organizing her thoughts when she writes.

Although her class participation demonstrates she understands the material, Jennifer lacks the basic EF skills needed for the writing process. Of course, this hampers her acquiring the higher-level writing techniques expected in middle school. Advancing her EF skills would unlock the considerable intellectual abilities she cannot currently display and extend.

The following table highlights the basic skills that need automaticity and the EF abilities required for different academic subjects.

Academic Area	Basic Skills Needed	Executive Functions Needed
Reading Comprehension	• Decoding: sounding out words • Reading fluency: speed and accuracy	• **Monitoring:** Checking for understanding as you read • **Shifting:** Understanding the author's and characters' points of view • **Time Management:** Budgeting time for reading and note-taking
Written Language	• Fine Motor skills: pencil grip, letter formation, use of space on a page • Writing fluency: speed and accuracy	• **Initiation:** Ability to start assignments. • **Planning:** Pre-writing (web or outline); Using words to guide a reader to a logical conclusion • **Shifting:** Thinking flexibly and anticipating a reader's reaction to your words • **Monitoring:** Assessing and editing your work • **Working Memory:** Keeping in mind writing skills.
Independent Studying, Homework, and Long-term Projects	• Using a planner • Bringing home needed materials • Having a set study time and place	• **Planning:** Envisioning short- and long-term tasks • **Shifting:** Transitioning from school to home, and completing your work independently • **Monitoring:** Assessing and editing your work • **Organizing Materials:** Gathering items for school, home, and play
Test-taking	• Knowing what to study • Ability to recall relevant information	• **Organizing Materials:** Making sure you have easy access to study guides and materials • **Planning:** Setting time to study before a test and managing time during a test • **Shifting:** Applying your knowledge to different contexts and integrating different ideas • **Monitoring:** Assessing and editing your work before turning it in

Introduction

To recap, EF describes the interrelated capacities used when we respond to, organize, and apply what we've learned—that is, when we interpret and act on information. The CEO-like EF capability of the brain coordinates a whole collection of interwoven powers for goal-directed, problem-solving action. Without its proper working, students have difficulty managing their thoughts, time, space, and materials in order to plan, begin, and complete projects.

Here's where self-regulation and social-emotional skills come to the forefront. Awareness and control of our thoughts, emotions, and behaviors let us quell impulses, delay gratification, and keep our focus; enabling us to read and accommodate to social cues from others. Without these components of EF, the best techniques, and the best minds, can't be fully deployed.

Since EF involves self-regulation and social-emotional skills, students without them often struggle socially, too. Difficulty thinking out of the box or seeing others' perspectives may make them miss the nuances of the slang and jokes of peers. Without a parent's intervention, their difficulty planning could lead to missed play dates. Equally, their inflexibility might incline them toward rigid insistence on certain activities, irritating their friends. And poor everyday problem-solving tactics might make them either give up too easily or adhere to a failing strategy.

That's why this workbook advances EF, a sense of self, and social-emotional skills simultaneously. Helping students understand how their overall approach to an assignment impacts its outcome goes a long way to solve the mystery of why their product doesn't match their knowledge and talents.

Self-Regulation Skills

How does this workbook advance self-regulated and socially adept learning as well as EF? Understanding **cognition, metacognition, and motivation**, the three main components of a self-regulated learner, is a good place to start.

The Components of Self-Regulation

Cognition

Cognition is thinking and acquiring knowledge—basically, learning. Teaching **cognitive strategies** gives learners a choice of tried-and-true study techniques such as connecting details to main points; rehearsing facts; summarizing in one's own words; organizing ideas; taking notes; using flashcards; employing imagery and mnemonics; and studying with a partner.

Metacognition

Metacognition is thinking about thinking. When students understand their learning style, along with the demands of a given task, they can pick the cognitive strategy that's best for them. With practice, they can use this metacognitive self-awareness to create a long-range plan, monitor its effectiveness, and adjust it as needed. Metacognitive tools include breaking down tasks into steps, creating checklists, and setting timers to help them progress through their plan. Yet one of the most effective metacognitive techniques is simply asking oneself questions as one follows basic action prompts.

Introduction

The Instructor Guide will detail the four metacognitive prompts you'll teach to fortify EF skills, but here's a brief preview:

1) Stop and Imagine
2) Think and Plan
3) Do and Review
4) Check and Turn In

Notice how each prompt in the following table includes follow-up questions for students to ask themselves. These prompts and questions guide them through an entire project. Notice also how this central, self-regulatory EF skill—working step by step to completion—extends a student's self-awareness and grasp of others' expectations.

EF Metacognitive Prompts

1 STOP and IMAGINE

WHAT DO I NEED TO DO?
- Stopping to think before you start saves time!
- Read the instructions carefully.
- Can you imagine what the work will look like when it is done? How will you feel?
- Do you know what to do and have the materials you need to do it?

2 THINK AND PLAN

HOW WILL I ACHIEVE MY GOAL?
- What steps will you follow to complete your goal?
- Create a step-by-step plan of action.
- Number the steps and estimate the time each will take to complete.
- Gather all the materials you need before you start.

3 DO AND REVIEW

FOLLOW THE PLAN.
- Follow your plan, stop, and review your work along the way.
- How are you doing?
- Does your work match the image you had? Do you need to adjust your plan?

4 CHECK AND TURN IN

DID I MEET MY GOAL?
- Make sure your work matches your goal.
- Don't forget the final step of turning it in!

Introduction

Notice, finally, that the first prompt reminds the student to **STOP** before jumping into a task. Impulsive students who rush to finish often perform surprisingly better when they simply slow down, read directions, break down the assignment into steps, and follow them in order. Equally, students who can't see the first step benefit from this initial prompt: stopping to break down a project into separate, small, easily understood steps to follow.

So **cognitive strategies** help students learn new material and **metacognitive strategies** help them start, monitor, and complete work. But what inspires them to use these great strategies? Here's where **motivation** comes in!

Motivation

Motivation is *why* we're willing to do something. It's the controlling force behind our actions because it initiates, guides, and maintains our goal-oriented behaviors. Motivation stems from self-awareness of what we want *most*, which often conflicts with other desires. For example, the immediate delight of texting a friend competes with the longer-lasting pleasure of finishing work. Students' considering and choosing their most desired outcome increase their motivation. This doesn't mean they'll never backslide, but it raises their engagement in the tasks that gain them the most, including persistently following an EF training plan. As students see that their work actually achieves what they aimed for, they experience both self-confidence and even more motivation.

Motivational strategies include building **self-awareness** (knowing one's own interests), developing **self-control** (focusing on those interests), and learning to **delay gratification** (putting off minor indulgences to get the big reward). So, you'd correctly

Introduction

predict that experiential self-awareness exercises would beef up the self-regulatory component of motivation. This EF workbook especially uses creative projective (self-revealing) interventions from the Oaklander Model to increase students' self-knowledge and confidence. The Instructor Guide covers her powerful method in greater depth, as do Karen Fried's works at karenfried.com, and the Student Workbook that follows. But here's a quick sketch of how the projective process in Oaklander's interventions empowers students' self-agency, letting them take in and employ new EF skills:

The Projective Process

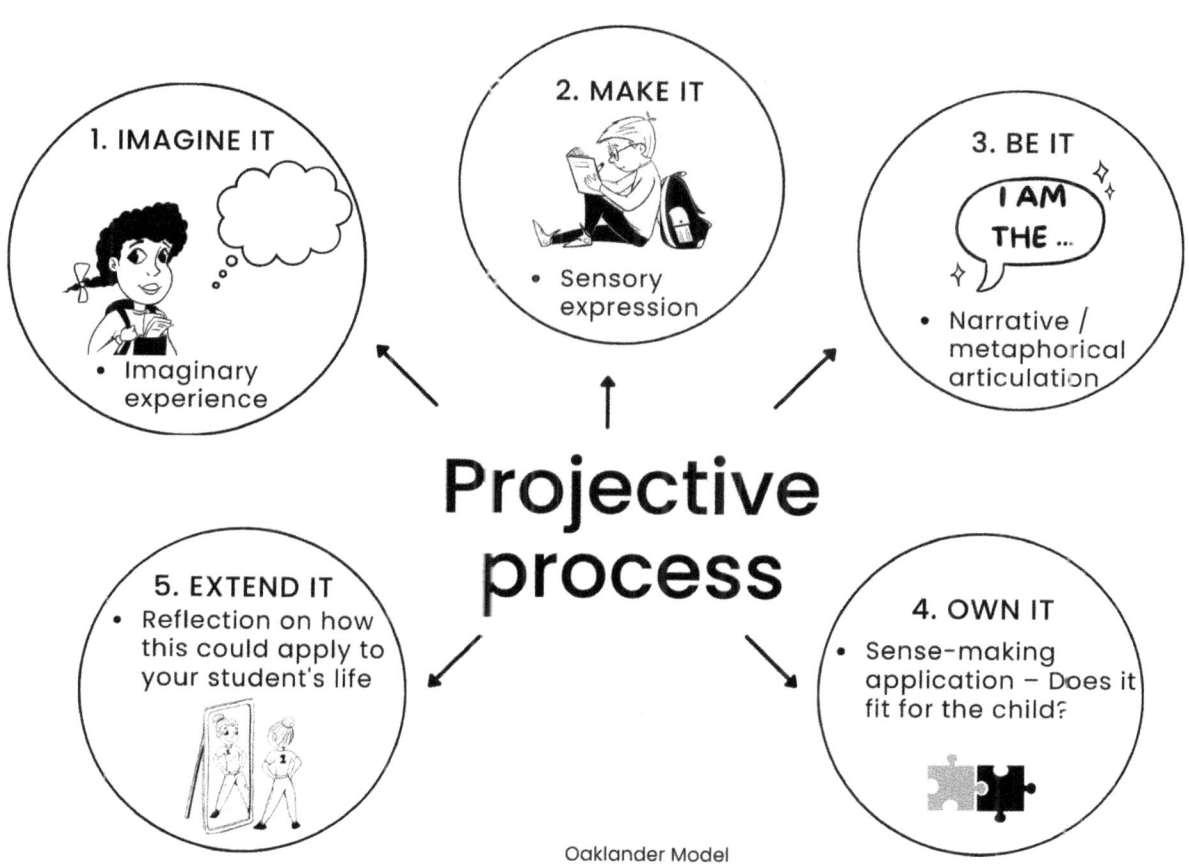

Oaklander Model

Introduction

1. **Imagine it.** Ask the student to imagine something they want.

2. **Make it.** Encourage the student to make it in some form that's fun for them: drawing, sand tray, clay, collage, storytelling or other medium.

3. **Be it.** Invite the student to become (act, make sounds, or speak as) a character or element in what they made.

4. **Own it.** Ask if the projection describes something true for them: "Does this fit for you?" Owning this projection of themself onto their creation will allow them to "try on" a new self-image or behavior in a fun, safe way.

5. **Extend it.** Gentle follow-up questioning about how the child might prefer the projected character, element, or situation to be can motivate them to enact a new self-image as a learner.

A short case study illustrates this projective process. An elementary-school girl at our Center who had difficulty reading presented with low motivation at the beginning of a session, saying, "I hate this, it's too hard to do all these exercises every time!"

The specialist then asked her to **imagine** that feeling, then **make** a drawing showing how she feels as a reader. The student drew a picture of a tiny child next to an enormous book. When asked to **be** the child in the drawing, she offered, "I am a very small child that can barely hold onto this big book!"

Following up, the specialist asked, "Does this fit for you? Do you feel like you're very small and barely holding onto a big book?" The student **owned** the projection, answering, "Yes! I hate reading, it's so hard for me—it always feels like I can't read the way I'm supposed to."

To help the girl **extend** it, the specialist now suggested, "OK, so if you could change this picture however you would like, how do you wish it could look?" The girl then drew a more in-perspective picture of a larger child with an appropriately sized book.

The specialist continued the projective process with a prompt: "Can you please **be** something in this picture?" Fully engaged, the girl exclaimed, "I am this girl holding a book that I can hold AND I can read!"

The specialist replied, "Wow! How can that happen in your life, do you think?" The girl answered, "I'll try a little harder when I'm here and maybe that will help."

In brief, the student depicted and located the source of her pain surrounding reading in her self-image as a non-reader. That self-awareness then let her imagine how she could change her view of herself, and create a new, helpful self-image that fueled her motivation.

Students who "hate school" often need to change their self-image, learn skills, and experience success before their motivation for learning can grow. So, it's crucial to deploy a multifaceted and sensitive approach to boosting EF skills, as this workbook does.

Introduction

Self-Control Strategies

A variety of stratagems exist to increase motivation by helping students reduce distractions interfering with the goal they themselves determined as their most desired. Researcher Angela Duckworth identified four key tactics for bolstering self-control:

- **Choose or change the situation.** Some settings are better for studying while others are better for socializing. If a student studies somewhere not conducive to work, teach the student to get up and find a new place.

- **Select what to pay attention to.** Modify the situation to eliminate items competing for the student's attention. For example, if the phone is distracting, get the student to move it!

- **Use Short-Cut Strategies.** Set up plans and prompts to link the study situation with desired actions, not distractions! For example, before leaving school, a student can create a study plan with a prompt: "When I get home I'll go to my room and study." The plan links getting home with studying; the choice avoids choosing instead to spend time on the phone. Even better, consistently linking plans with good outcomes forms great new habits and increases motivation.

- **Change the way you think.** When situations and temptations cannot be changed, students can still change the way they think. For instance, students try harder when they *change how they interpret frustration* from being a sign of failure to being a sign they're challenging themselves.

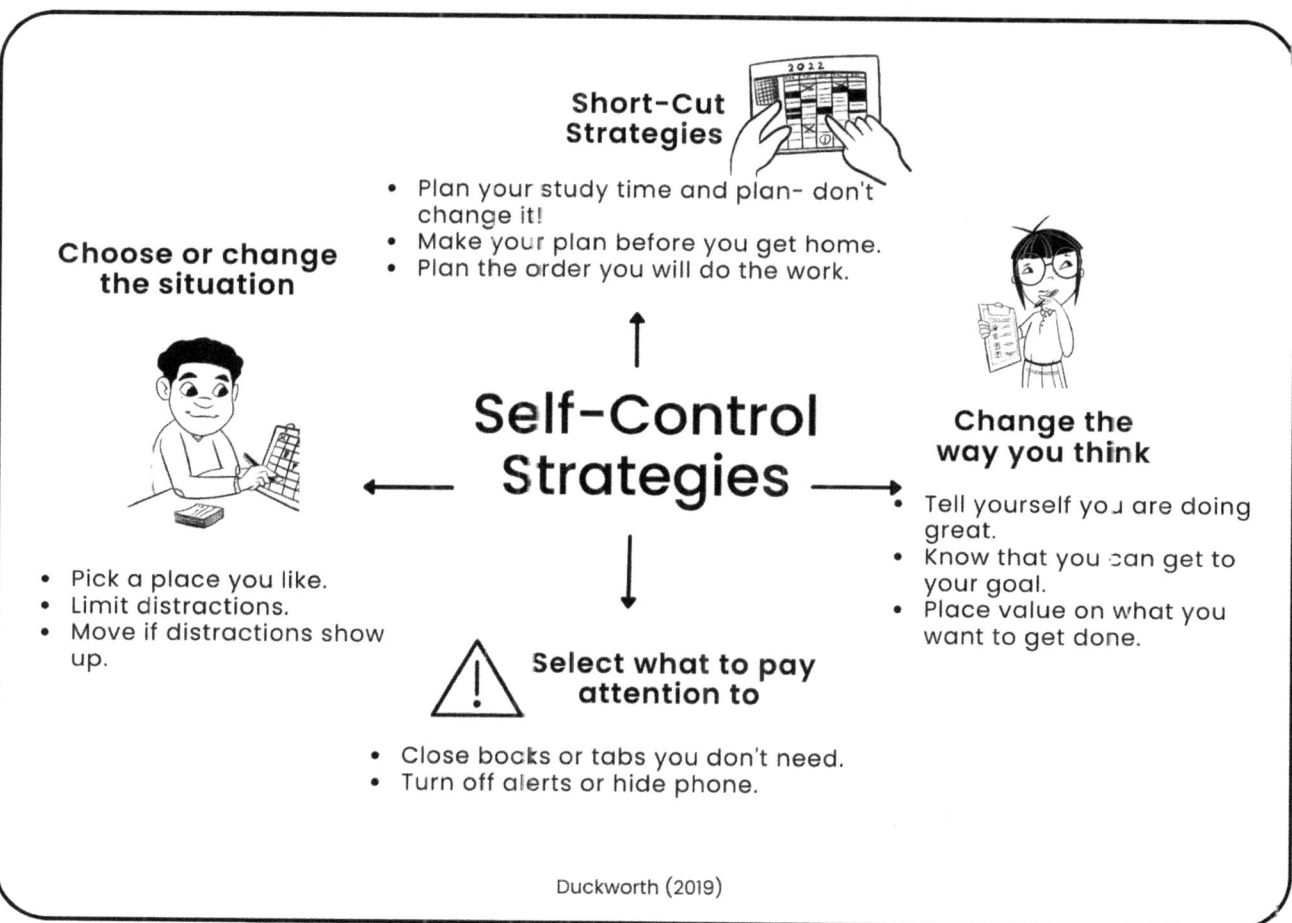

Duckworth (2019)

Delay Gratification Strategies

Other aids to motivation abound. Learning to **delay gratification** greatly alters student behavior. Students can learn to compare the value of indulging an immediate temptation versus the value of completing their work. They can also learn it's their choice to get their homework done *now* rather than talking to their friend *now*.

The saying that "nothing succeeds like success" is true, so setting students up for success will further strengthen Executive Functioning and self-regulation skills. Change may be difficult at first, but it becomes easier with each new victory.

Introduction

Social-Emotional Skills

Social-emotional skills allow students to connect with others, control their emotions and react appropriately. These skills help students build positive relationship and make appropriate decisions. This workbook uses the Oaklander model to help students build their social-emotional skills.

Key Concepts of this Program

You saw that many students with weak EF also have a poor sense of self and connection to others. That's why this program integrates and advances the whole child's self-regulatory, social-emotional, cognitive, and metacognitive capacities to help them take control of learning.

How to Begin

As noted, a student's becoming aware of their thought processes and of the feelings surrounding them empowers them to expand their EF abilities. So, at the very start of the program each participant takes a quiz to discover their EF strengths and weaknesses, and you'll also interview them to confirm what each requires. You can then mine the workbook for activities focusing on specific EF areas and use them at any time, repeat as often as needed, and modify as desired to meet each student's particular learning profile.

To do so, this whole child EF program integrates two equally crucial types of learning tools:

- **Executive Functioning** to build independent learning abilities

- **Oaklander Model and Self-Regulation Strategies** to build self-awareness and social-emotional skills, and thus enable self-regulation and relation to others

Now you're ready to get acquainted with the **Instructor Guide** and the **Student Workbook** through the brief roadmap below. The **Instructor Guide** shows specialists, step by step, how to build students' EF powers though EF strategies along with self-regulatory and social-emotional activities—the EF and Oaklander-style tools this program blends. The Instructor Guide first details the **EF metacognitive prompts** you'll use to teach each EF ability. Then it summarizes the **Oaklander Model** so you can employ its creative, client-led activities to heighten students' self-awareness and social-emotional capacities, and thus their self-regulation. In addition, the Guide's unit on **Preparing the Sessions** goes from the first to the last sessions and specifies meeting setup, purpose, process, and progress assessment.

Students should have their own copy of the Student Workbook to write in. As mentioned, the first unit comprises an EF Quiz and lets participants set their own goals based on it. After this first foray into self-awareness, you'll guide them through five units covering the metacognitive prompts until they become habitual and students do them independently: **STOP and IMAGINE; THINK and PLAN; DO and REVIEW; CHECK and TURN IN.** A bonus **REASSESS** unit lets them gauge their progress and set new goals.

Instructor Guide

Teaching Executive Functioning Skills

As mentioned, students will take the Executive Functioning Quiz in Unit 1, to discover areas they're strong in and ones that need attention—and to get used to reflecting on themselves, a crucial skill for life and for learning. Once they've taken the EF Quiz, they themselves can determine which abilities to concentrate on through specific activities and exercises in the workbook. As you work through each unit, you'll find that using shorthand for the prompts—STOP, THINK, DO, CHECK—makes them easy for students to recall. The chart below notes the key EF skills for each of the STOP, THINK, DO, and CHECK prompts.

Instructor Guide

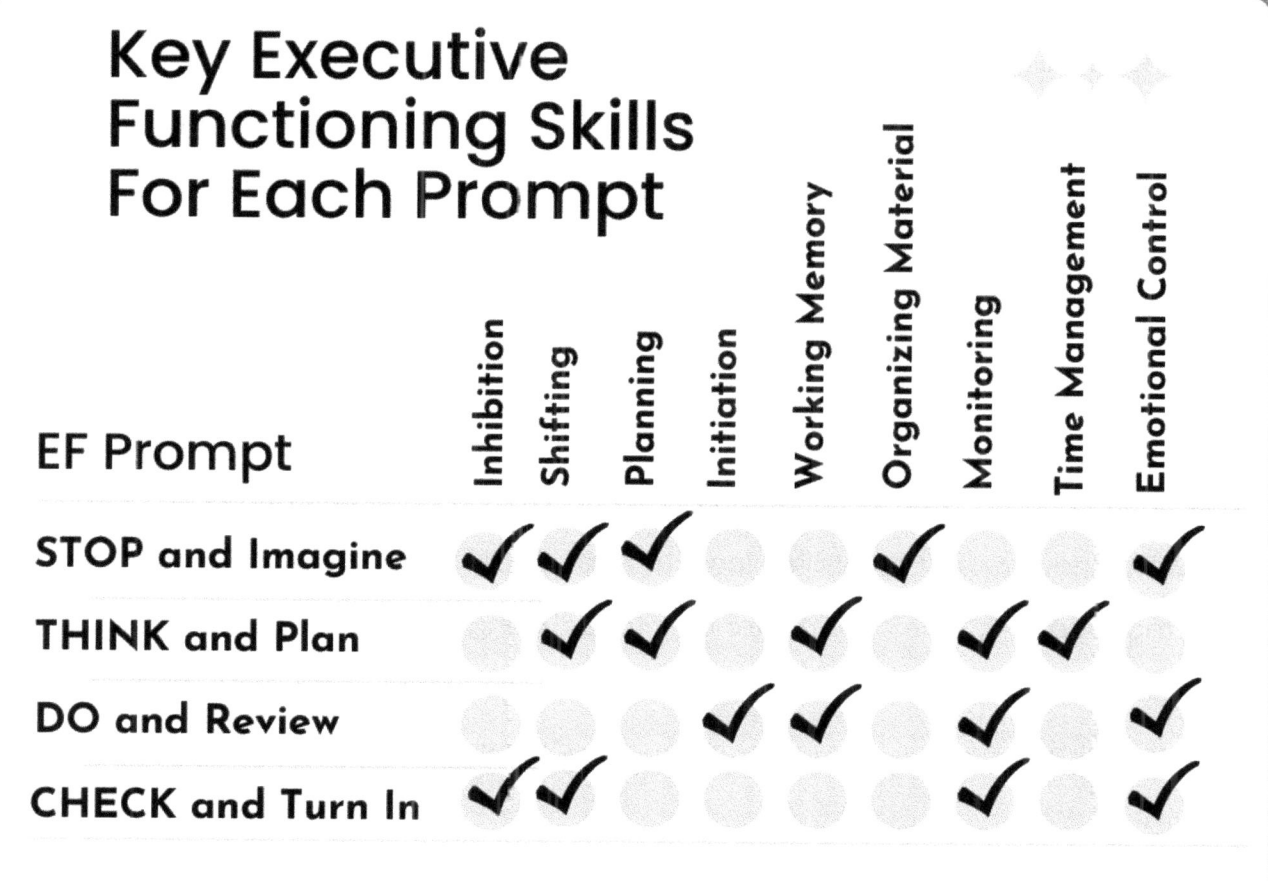

You'll cover the metacognitive prompts one at a time, but here's a comprehensive view of the prompts, their links to self-awareness and social connectivity, and their order in the process of working independently:

- The **STOP and IMAGINE** unit proves the power of simply *pausing* before starting work. Stopping lets students become aware of feelings surrounding schoolwork—the first step in learning to regulate emotions, thoughts, and behavior so they can identify and commit to their goals. Then they're ready to imagine (visualize precisely) *what* they need to do to meet those goals and exactly *how* they're going to do it.

Instructor Guide

For many, learning to STOP is the hardest part of the program. So, you may find that starting sessions with a STOP and IMAGINE activity greatly raises productivity. Specifically, having students take time to understand directions, organize their thoughts and feelings, and clear out and restock their backpack and desk sets them up for success.

- Once students routinely STOP to organize their thoughts, feelings, materials, and spaces, and then IMAGINE their aims, they can tackle the **THINK and PLAN** unit. It outlines how to craft a detailed long-term plan using checklists and a daily planner to manage their time and master their focus. Along with these concrete, good-habit-forming organizational strategies, the unit presents useful short-term (or working) memory tips that increase students' sense of control over immediate tasks.

- Next, the **DO and REVIEW** unit details the actions required to follow the learner's plan. It will also guide preparation for and performance on tests and presentations, because doing assignments independently demands and sharpens the same abilities needed for written or spoken exams:
  - Breaking down complex projects into manageable, logically ordered steps
  - Correctly estimating how long each step will take
  - Starting, stopping, and changing activities as the plan requires
  - Using short-term Working Memory

- At this point the **CHECK and TURN IN** unit provides concrete ways students can make sure their finished work matches their goal. Its strategies let students monitor their efforts and their products' quality in relation to available time and curricular expectations. Practicing these techniques with you until they're automatic creates proficiency, and pride, in working independently.

- The bonus **REASSESS** unit offers students the opportunity to assess how much they've learned from the program, and what new goals they'd like to take on. They'll also see that they can always improve old skills and create new ones to work even more effectively—another leap in awareness of their own, and others', expectations.

Teaching Social-Emotional and Self-Regulation Skills

Understanding and Using Oaklander Model Activities

Integral to this workbook's whole child approach is the work of Violet Oaklander, a child and adolescent therapist who applied the principles of relational, projective, "here-and-now" Gestalt Therapy to work with youngsters (for an analysis of her thought and method, see more at oaklandertraining.org). Her classic 1978 *Windows to Our Children* has been translated into 16 languages and is used worldwide. You have already read a dramatic example of her process in the short case study given above, which demonstrates the centrality of a child's self-concept in the experience of learning challenges, and how remediating that sense of self opens the path to strengthening EF.

Oaklander began her career as a special education teacher. At that time the "best practice" for children with attentional or processing difficulties was to severely limit distractions, to the point of setting them up in a completely undecorated room. Oaklander rejected this spartan environment, feeling that all children—even her special needs students—learn and thrive in vibrant surroundings that stimulate rather than shutter their connection with their senses, body, emotions, and intellect. So, she filled her classroom with color from student drawings, music from her guitar as she taught spelling, and soft and coarse manipulatives awakening their sense of touch. Oaklander's students moved their bodies to learn with dance, jumping, and physical freedom. Soon her colleagues and principal started visiting her noisy, colorful classroom to see why her children were excelling. Oaklander began mentoring other teachers, and later became a psychotherapist.

Her incorporation of projective Gestalt theory and interventions into client-led play therapy became known as the "Oaklander Model." She characterized it as creating "a way of talking about things that is very safe, and then gradually bringing it back ... to give [children and adolescents] experience with parts of themselves that they no longer own or experience." That is, as a youngster's sense of self increases, so does the ability to access blocked parts of that self, including emotions and intellect.

Equally important, the sense of self blossoms through an authentic relationship between the child and the specialist, teacher or counselor. Drawing on philosopher Martin Buber's core value, the "I-Thou relationship" (1958), Oaklander knew that mutually respectful, honest connection with another promotes the child's confidence and facilitates learning, and so is key in teaching as in therapy. She understood that establishing what Buber called an authentic relationship—genuine, direct, specific to the individuals—is the essential foundation for work with children. Nothing happens without it, and it needs to be nurtured. So, a teacher must meet the student as two separate individuals, neither superior to the other. This means that when interacting with even the youngest child, the teacher accepts that student's current, real self. And the model's inviting activities perfectly (if at first unconsciously) demonstrate—project—the youngster's current, real self.

In our experience—the K&M Center has used this approach since 1994—the Oaklander Model's authentic engagement with each youngster maximizes the benefits of EF training because the trusting specialist-student bond built opens your student to a new view of themselves as a learner, and so to new learning strategies.

Applied to academic areas, the Oaklander Model connects young people with their intellect and unlocks the skills they need to learn. Using playful, hands-on media such as picture cards, drawing materials, clay, collage, puppets, and a sand tray filled with miniature toys lowers students' resistance to confronting their learning or attentional difficulties, and emboldens them to try new tacks. When combined with best practices from current learning EF theory, this model provides teachers, counselors, and educational specialists accessible, fun, and effective instructional techniques.

Projective Exercises: Definition and Purpose

Imaginative activities and artwork display what's on the youthful creator's mind, even if unconsciously; gentle follow-up questions help them recognize and explore those feelings and thoughts. So projective exercises:

1. Allow children to access and express their feelings.
2. Strengthen their sense of self as they create images, talk about them, and finally interpret their meaning (in Oaklander's term, "own the projection").

Instructor Guide

Your Role in Using the Oaklander Model

As you've probably guessed, the instructor's attitude is central to this relationship-based approach. Let's specify its elements:

- **Be present:** Bring yourself fully to the session and your student. Leave outside concerns, outside.
- **Connect:** Understand the student's experience in working with you, while retaining your role as an educational specialist. Honor how they see themselves as a learner, while retaining your knowledge of their challenges and vision of their potential.
- **Confirm:** Validate your student's potential at that moment and for the long term. That is, accept where they are, yet maintain the image of their eventual success.
- Use **genuine and full communication**: Be genuine and honest in your communication with the student.
- Follow a **credo of respect:** Meet the child at the child's level, respect their rhythm, be present, honor and value the child and the parents as worthy human beings.

What to Watch for in Your Student

As you apply the model, look for markers of your student's maturity and blockages. Developmental issues affect how children function across the board, not just academically. To survive, cope, and get needs met, a child with an immature sense of self may anesthetize the senses, restrict the body, block emotions, close the intellect, or adopt inappropriate behaviors. Watch for these areas of concern in your sessions:

- **Struggle for self:** The newborn gets their sense of self from the primary caregiver—their voice, touch, face. Yet the growing child struggles against this merging in order to individuate (define the self as unique and separate). Successful individuation marks maturity.

- **Egocentricity:** The child, especially when very young, is cognitively and emotionally unable to comprehend external, separate experience. Thus, the child blames the self for any trauma experienced.

- **Introjects:** Lacking the maturity and cognitive capacity to reject or ignore hurtful or inaccurate descriptions of the self, the young child accepts negative or wrong characterizations and develops a faulty belief system about themself.

- **Getting needs met:** Children will try anything to get basic needs (acceptance, love, being heard) met and to avoid rejection and abandonment—including inappropriate behaviors or symptoms.

- **Expressing emotions:** Many children have learned early that expressing emotions, particularly anger, is unacceptable. Oaklander Model activities provide healthy ways to recognize and convey blocked emotions.

- **Limit-setting:** For the health and safety of the young person, instructors and parents must set limits. Acceptance of the need for limits—like for rules in a game—is a mark of maturity.

- **Cultural expectations:** Children quickly learn what's expected of them based upon the culture of their particular group. Conflicting messages and tensions can arise when they also grow up in a second, different culture.

Instructor Guide

- **System expectations:** Many systems besides the family affect a child's development, including schools, medical or religious institutions, sports teams, and other social groups. Observe your student's awareness and management of these expectations.

Oaklander Model Terms for EF Training

- **Contact:** Being in contact means being fully present with all aspects of the self—physical senses, emotions, and intellect. Healthy infants are born with a capacity to be in contact. But children who experience difficulties may lose their ability to access one or more of these elements of the self. Most students who come to our learning center have lost contact with their intellect in one or more areas of cognitive processing, which inhibits their use of Executive Functioning skills.

- **Sense of self:** Children with a clear sense of self are aware of their body, emotions, and intellect. They know if they can sit still and listen to a lesson or learn best with tactile or kinesthetic reinforcement or occasional movement breaks. Students with a robust sense of self can also self-regulate when experiencing strong emotions and can tolerate frustration; those with an immature sense of self require external support and opportunities to learn self-regulation skills. Figuring out how they live as well as how they learn gives youngsters awareness of their strengths and weaknesses as students. That is, understanding their own physical, emotional, and intellectual contact functions enables them to use targeted strategies, get support as needed, and become confident, capable students.

- **Resistance:** Children and adolescents naturally defend themselves against an experience in which they don't feel supported. Conversely, Oaklander reminded us, a child's showing no resistance "can be a sign that her sense of self is so fragile that she must do whatever she is told to do in order to feel that she can survive." Teachers and all adults need to keep in mind that young persons' resistance is their way of protecting themselves, and deserves to be honored—that is, not pushed against or denied, but acknowledged by dropping the problematic activty for a time. Struggling learners especially may resist helpful interventions from nstructors, saying, "I'm fine, I don't need this help" or "I already tried that with my teacher/tutor/mom and it didn't work." These comments show they're resistant to a new technique for fear they will again fail and have to face weaknesses in their learning profile. When their resistance is acknowledged and respected, students may be more willing to risk new or retry old strategies.

- **Awareness:** Applying this approach strengthens children's sense of self as students by helping them become aware of—in contact with—their own learning process. That is, it lets them answer questions that have probably been troubling them: How do I learn? What are my strengths and weaknesses as a student? How do I manage challenges? How do I respond to others who are there to help me learn?

- **Senses and the body:** Interventions involving the physical aspect of the whole child allow each to develop contact with their five senses as well as to experience sensations in their bodies. Many children lodge stress from school in their bodies and may block awareness of that bodily stress. Interventions in this model pointedly redress their loss of contact with senses and the body:

- **Touch:** finger painting, using clay, sand tray, textures of manipulable
- **Sight:** looking at pictures, kaleidoscopes
- **Hearing:** painting while listening to music; using musical instruments
- **Taste:** mindfulness exercises such as tasting segments of an orange and comparing that taste with the teacher's description; talking about favorite and not-so-favorite tastes
- **Smell:** experiencing different scents of flowers, fruit, grass
- **The body:** doing fun activities in the session to heighten awareness of their body; games like Charades, Simon Says, and puppet shows; learning to attend to their breath as a clue to their internal states

- **Self-Regulation:** Children of any age seek emotional *homeostasis*—constant re-balancing—in response to stress. Those with learning and attentional issues usually experience anxiety or anger in the learning environment and may employ inappropriate behaviors such as acting out or withdrawing. EF, self-regulatory, and social-emotional skills help them acknowledge and manage their emotions so they can focus on the task at hand.

- **Emotions:** Emotional expression work allows children to find and support their true self by helping them understand what feelings are, discover their own feelings—especially if these have been blocked—and express them safely. Creative projective modalities (drawing, clay, puppets, sand tray scenes, storytelling, music, play-acting) facilitate this work.

The Process: Using the Oaklander Model to Strengthen EF

First, establish the relationship. It's essential that you build a sense of safety and trust and accomplish the tasks you've laid out in each session, since calm and predictability relieve the student's anxiety and encourage involvement in new tactics. Continually evaluate a student's ability to be present the whole time you're working together. When a child loses contact, which can appear as resistance, fading energy or spacing out, that's your cue to take a break or find another activity to re-engage the child. Again, it's all about the presence of both of you during your session.

Next, gauge the student's readiness to use projective techniques. Continue to assess the student's interest and energy to engage throughout the session. At each step throughout this process, watch for resistance: Observe body language and other evidence of affect (stiffening, losing focus, deflective behaviors). If resistance emerges, respect it and move to another activity until the youngster is ready.

Recall, though, that an overly agreeable child or adolescent may not know themself well enough to make choices based on a strong sense of self and may just go along with everything. If your student seems out of contact with their intellect, or is very young, they may not understand what you're asking or may not feel enough support to express their preference. Watch for patterns, themes, polarities, and stuck places as you assess the child.

Building awareness through the senses (touch, sight, hearing, smell, and taste), body movement, emotional expression, and intellectual stimulation helps children stay in contact with themselves and present in sessions. When children become anxious they restrict or inhibit these vital contact functions. So, energizing these aspects of the whole child is a primary goal in the Oaklander Model and in this EF training process. Copied here for your convenience, this graphic depicts the 5 stages of student involvement in a projective activity. Now we can describe the technique in greater detail since it reveals both your built connection and the student's readiness to work with self-image. Look for the youngster's willingness to engage.

The Projective Process

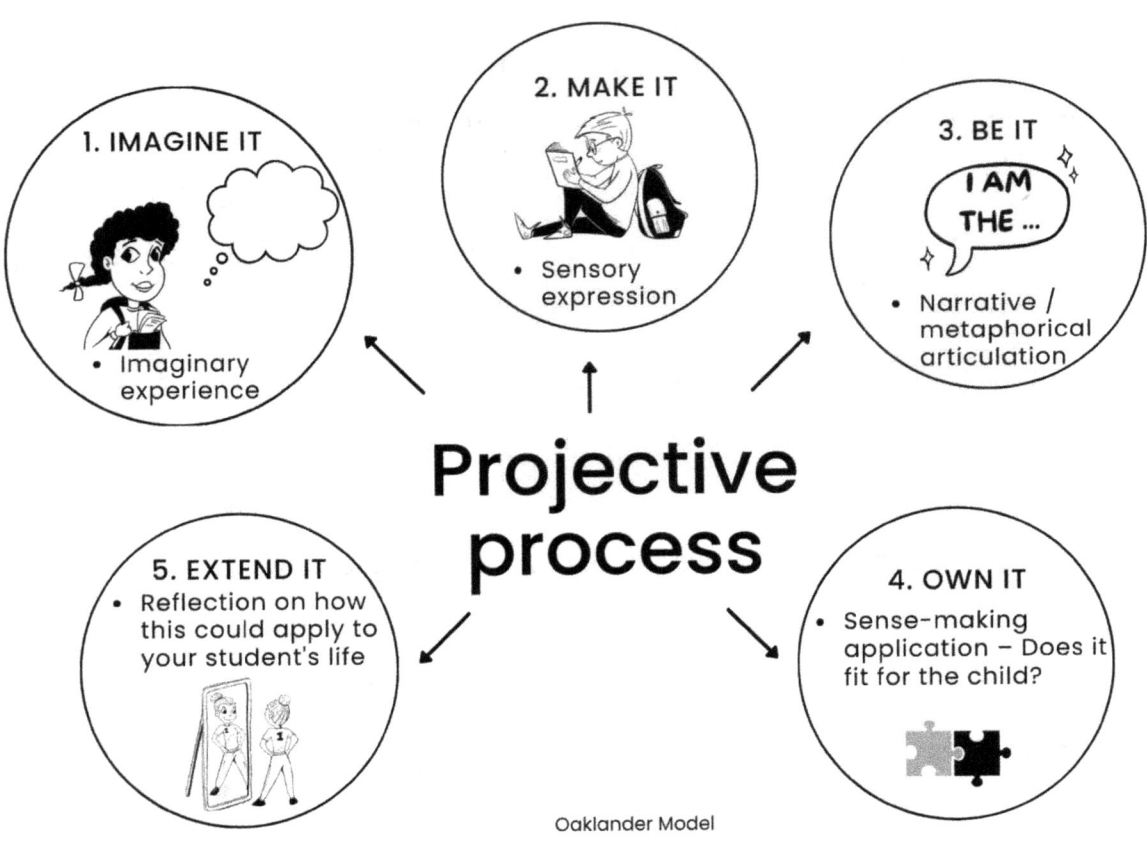

Oaklander Model

- **Do a projective activity** (drawing, clay, puppets, sand tray, storytelling)
- **Tell you about what they produced** (how they did it or how it felt to do it—that is, sharing the experience by talking about it)

- **Enter the metaphor or image** ("become" part of the creation; able to "be" a created object or character; filling it in with details)
- **See the depicted situation** from the perspective of an object, character, or part of it
  - Able to answer, "Which one is you?" and "Describe yourself."
  - Dialoging with an object, character, or part. Able to answer, "What's going on? What's happening?" and to tell the story.
- **Own the projection** at either of two levels:
  - **Symbolic level:** The young person can tell about the situation, but only as metaphor. That is, the internal and external meanings are not yet integrated.
  - **Reality level:** The child or adolescent realizes that what's experienced within the metaphor is also experienced by them in real life. Making this connection deepens the work and allows what has been out of awareness to come into awareness. Asking, "Do you feel that way?" can move the young person into this deeper level of work.

Understanding how these two areas—weak contact with one's feelings and thoughts and an unclear sense of self—hobble EF helps parents and educational professionals support the youngster's developing those qualities. Creating a structured, clear treatment plan, and explaining it to adults for whom you have releases, helps everyone understand the session goals.

The Treatment Plan: Blending Oaklander Model and EF Training

Your treatment plan is based upon careful assessment of the student's self-concept, social-emotional skills, and learning profile. It aims to achieve specific goals set by the parent, teacher, and student. While individually tailored, all treatment plans:

Instructor Guide

Understand the student's starting point.

- **Contact skills** of looking, listening, tasting, touching, smelling, moving, and talking. If the student has difficulty making contact, you can provide these experiences through fun activities suited to the child, such as games involving auditory processing, visual processing, storytelling, or tactile/kinesthetic movement.
- **Learning profile,** typically done through educational testing, neuropsychological testing, teacher reports, parent reports and most importantly self-report from the student about their learning strengths, weaknesses, and goals.
  - Identify areas of EF strength and weakness through the K&M Executive Functioning (EF) Quiz in Unit 1, along with the developmental evaluation detailed above.
  - Share results with the student, in developmentally appropriate and comprehensible language, as well as with parents and teachers. This knowledge establishes your relationship on honesty and trust, strengthens the student's sense of self, empowers them as a partner in their remedial work, and lets you discover their goals.

Assess and address resistance as noted above by observing behavioral indicators that the student is approaching a "pain point" or area of weakness in the process of remediating underlying learning difficulties. Recall that resistance has been a useful (if temporary) way they avoided or coped with these weaknesses, but that your work offers more effective tools for handling those challenges. As you saw earlier in the case of the girl who drew herself as tiny compared to a gigantic book, students who "hate school" must come to believe they can overcome their failures before they can engage in learning.

- **Strengthen the student's sense of self** through your specific, honest, and accepting I-Thou relationship, which allows them to express their self as separate and unique. Exercises that affirm who they are and who they are not, all fortify the self in the sessions.

- **Address and correct negative self-perception:** Drawing or otherwise representing parts of the child's self they don't like, anger work, and self-nurturing work allow them to reveal and reintegrate hated aspects of themself through understanding and compassion. Recognizing and loving these parts, rather than continuing to buy into faulty negative characterizations imbibed in childhood, lets youngsters replace self-critical "I should" and "I ought" thoughts with self-nurturing "I want" statements.

- **Increase the student's self-awareness:** Projective techniques invite awareness. This is another lesson from the brief case study of the girl who first drew herself as dwarfed by a huge book but left with a hopeful drawing of herself as a successful reader—and a realistic plan for realizing that new self-vision.

Build Executive Functioning skills by practicing following metacognitive prompts and creating checklists of logically ordered, doable steps in a project. The six units of the Student Workbook abound with varied, effective strategies students can make "second nature" as they achieve learning independence.

Parent Communication Starts at Intake

As part of the intake process, prioritize your relationship with parents. Clear, respectful communication establishes a trusting connection between educators and parents, just as between educators and students. A transparent, understandable treatment plan with explicitly stated goals everyone agrees on, and regular progress updates, are other central components of your relationship with parents.

Discuss boundaries regarding time and fee; safety and office rules; and ethical and legal considerations and lay them out both in writing and conversations. Basic points to clarify with parents include:

Respecting Session Time Limits

Tardiness to sessions jeopardizes treatment goals not just by losing time but by producing anxiety as you rush to complete tasks. It also telegraphs disrespect for the student's process.

- Similarly, outline in your discussion exactly when sessions end and when you are available for consultation, so parents don't feel they may regularly speak to you after the sessions, "Just for a minute."

Expectations

You want parents to clearly understand the treatment plan and the progress of their child. Early on, set a session with parents to clarify any part of your work they don't understand so they become integral partners in their child's sessions.

For parents who have unrealistic expectations about your work, you may start your conversation this way:

- "As you know, I'm using the Oaklander Model to help [child's name] improve [his/her/their] Executive Functioning skills for school and everyday life. Violet Oaklander often said, 'I don't fix kids' as though they are 'problems' needing to be fixed. I follow her lead and, like her, I want to strengthen [child's name] sense of self and awareness of [his/her/their] own feelings and thoughts, so [he/she/they] can learn independently."

Then, explain how your treatment plan has succeeded thus far, and how it aims to achieve the goal of making the child an independent learner. That is, educate parents on what you **will** do for their youngster:

- Help the child feel better about themself as a learner.
- Explain how they learn and why they're struggling and teach them how to use their intellect to show what they're capable of.
- Help them find appropriate ways to cope with schoolwork and with stress around their learning deficits. Let them experience emotions about school that are now blocked so they can manage them better.
- Discuss expectations and boundaries for acceptable behavior, and the consequences of disrespectful behavior.
  - Give them the language to express themselves.
  - Reflect on their behavior whenever they cross boundaries.
  - Address problematic behavioral situations by coming up with a plan of action that they and adults in charge understand and accept.
- Work with them to set a clear plan for completing and turning in assignments.

Preparing the Sessions

Setting and Sharing Session Purpose and Process

Individualize Aims and Tools for Each Session

Enabling a student to work independently at their potential requires individualized instruction in each session. Follow the treatment plan you tailored to that youngster's needs and abilities but remain open to adjusting the plan as needed.

Instructor Guide

As you design each session plan, keep in mind the student's learning style, and choose specific tools and activities that capitalize on their strengths and remediate deficits. At the same time, be responsive to the child's expressed aims.

Set and Share Goals for Each Session

Share session plan notes with parents and professionals for whom you have releases. In age-appropriate terms, state session goals to your student at the start of each session and review your progress in them just before the session ends.

Envision Expanded Goals

- Recall that you're building your students' skills for now and for the future. You're not just teaching for a test; you're teaching skills for any test. With your help, students learn more than how to compensate for or "work around" a learning difficulty; you're constructing underlying skills for learning and for life. In the bonus REASSESS unit, students will practice setting new goals for themselves on their own. But from the very first session, you'll be holding in your mind how everything they learn will make greater and greater aims accessible to them.

For the First and All Sessions

Once you've assessed a child and made a treatment plan, it's time to start work. **The initial session sets the tone** for the whole program. Here are its primary elements:

The Relationship

As you know, your very first step is to establish and constantly nourish a mutually respectful and honest rapport. You'll do so through ...

- **your consistent presence** with and for the child. Neither of you checks phones or multi-tasks. You're calmly present with the child even—especially—when they are stressed, avoidant, withdrawn, or angry.

- **confirming the student's value** by holding your vision of their potential even—again, especially—when they're struggling. You ask about and validate their own goals.

- **clarity,** so the student knows what needs to be learned and the strategies you provide for learning it. State your (reachable) expectations for them at the start, during, and after this and all sessions.

- **showing that the child matters to you** before, during, and after sessions by recalling (or jotting down post-session) anything important to them which they shared with you.

- **presenting time and behavioral boundaries as beneficial to the child** by keeping sessions fully for their use, and safe.

Student Motivation

Ensure that the student is on board and interested in the program:
- Explain why they're there—that is, demystify the process. Don't assume they're clear on why they're receiving educational help from you, even if it was explained. This is important because:
    - They probably aren't sure why they're here or how coming will help them.
    - They'd rather be doing something else.

Instructor Guide

- They probably have extremely negative assumptions about why they're coming for help.
- Talking about their learning style encourages metacognition (thinking about thinking)—a type of self-awareness which makes trying new techniques feel less random and more hopeful.

- Assure them your work together will make schoolwork easier and more enjoyable and will let them learn better. This assurance develops a sense of purpose that helps overcome resistance.
- Make the session fun and engaging:
  - Include exercises with toys, drawing, funny or interesting writing prompts.
  - Divide this and all sessions into many activities to refresh student interest.
  - Build and maintain their physical, emotional, and intellectual contact functions in this as in every session.
  - Show your energy and enthusiasm for learning to help the child "catch" it.

Student Choices

- Youngsters' sense of self is strengthened when they weigh options and express preferences. Offer them an appropriate level of agency in sessions by asking:
  - "What do you want to do first?"
  - "When do you want to have game time?"
  - "What do you want to write about?"
  - "What are positive ways you can take control here? In school? At home?"

Student Mastery

Find ways to convey a feeling of success, to facilitate both self-awareness and motivation.

- Set up your sessions to enable them to complete at least one activity to their satisfaction.
- Acknowledge their completion of each exercise throughout the session.
- Ask about an academic or life skill they mastered previously.
- Ask about accomplishments they've experienced lately at home, in sports, in music, or in social groups.

Generalization

- Students in later stages of educational therapy will have seen that the specific concepts you cover in sessions generalize, or apply to, their schoolwork. Plant the seed of that discovery right from the start.
- Your continued communication with parents, teachers, and any other professionals working with the child ensures consistency across home, school, and other settings.

Assessing Progress

The best way to measure progress is to check in with the child, parent, and teachers. But you can start that check-in from the get-go in the first session. Have them compare how they're working now to how they worked last year. If things are tougher for them, help them reframe that perception by exploring the increased complexity

Instructor Guide

of the material and demands on their time management and independent effort—exactly what your work together will help them handle.

Now you may congratulate yourself on **your own progress** in working through this Introduction and Instructor Guide! You are now ready to look over the Student Workbook so you can help youngsters develop a strong sense of self, greater social-emotional capacities, and robust Executive Functioning skills.

Review: Points to Keep in Mind

- Before every session, remind yourself why you're doing this program, and keep that big picture in mind.
- Share that end goal with your learner by keeping dialogue about the program open with them: "Why are we doing this?"
- Track what's going on in school as well as in sessions, so students connect what they're learning with you to what they're learning in class.
- Remember that nothing succeeds like success. Take "baby steps" as needed to ensure comprehension and mastery of each task or skill.
- Celebrate even little victories!
- Monitor behavior: Pause to praise improved behavior as well as to discuss any negative behavior.
- Explain and re-explain the student's learning profile whenever needed. But avoid using educational/ability labels: You want every student to know and define themself in their own terms.
- Envision your student's potential even while remediating their current challenges. You want them to "catch" that expanded vision of themselves.

Student Workbook

Goal of the Workbook

The goal of this workbook is to teach you how to build Executive Functioning (EF) skills so you can take control of your schoolwork. The Executive Functioning Program presented here increases your ability to plan, start, and finish tasks. It strengthens the neurological (brain) activity that supports Executive Functioning by helping you pinpoint your goals and challenges, build thinking skills to meet them, and practice efficient organizational strategies. In other words, the program boosts your productivity and independence by developing useful habits for identifying, advancing, and completing your aims. Achieving your goals involves a whole series of smaller tasks, so the more you exercise your Executive Functioning habits of planning, starting, and finishing, the easier and quicker you can accomplish what you want.

What is Executive Functioning?

Executive Functioning is the umbrella term for a wide range of skills that work together as the CEO, or manager, of your brain. Executive Functioning skills allow a person to look at a task, understand the directions, gather needed materials, estimate the time it will take, begin the task, finish it, check it over, and turn it in. Everyone uses those abilities every day—not just for schoolwork—so building Executive Functioning skills is worth the effort for anyone at any age. But since schoolwork involves a lot of tasks, powering up your Executive Functioning skills will clearly pay off for you right now.

Student Workbook

Executive Functioning Components

Inhibition: The ability to stop off-task actions.	The ability to STOP is critical to building all the other Executive Functioning skills. People who react automatically miss the chance to assess a situation accurately and to attack a job efficiently.
Shifting: The ability to transition from one activity to another or a way of thinking about or doing something in another way.	People with Executive Functioning difficulties often say they don't do well with transitions. Adjusting to a new schedule, project, and even home routine requires the Executive Functioning skill called "shifting."
Emotional Control: The ability to regulate emotional responses to stress.	Emotional Control requires the ability to stop and think about what you're feeling and what your wisest reaction would be. The ability to calm yourself and to focus on your desired outcome will help you attain your goal
Monitoring: The ability to judge the quantity and quality of one's work based on expected standards.	Monitoring means checking the quality and pace of work. Monitoring your work lets you know if you're on track to complete the task in time and if you are doing it correctly.
Organizing Materials: The ability to organize objects in work, play, and storage areas.	Organizing your materials helps you keep track of what you have and what you need. Students who struggle with organization often have trouble finding items they need quickly and turning in assignments on time.
Working Memory: The ability to remember information for immediate use.	Working Memory is the ability to keep a small amount of information—a sentence or digits in a phone number—in your mind long enough to use it right away. Your Working Memory has a limit, so if it is overloaded it may lose information.
Time Management: Allotting appropriate time for each task.	Time management means knowing how long something will take and planning the time necessary to complete it.
Planning: The ability to manage tasks by setting goals and developing steps to achieve the goals.	Planning is the ability to create a path to get from where you are to where you want to be. Taking a large project and breaking it down into doable steps help you complete the project. Having a plan saves time since you'll know exactly what you need to do every time you start work
Initiation: The ability to get started on tasks without many prompts and cues	Initiation requires overcoming procrastination and starting work even if it is something you don't want to do. Nailing your THINK AND PLAN Executive Functioning skills makes you organized and confident, which encourages getting it done!

Academic Area	Basic Skills Needed	Executive Functions Needed
Reading Comprehension	• Decoding: sounding out words • Reading fluency: speed and accuracy	• **Monitoring:** Checking for understanding as you read • **Shifting:** Understanding the author's and characters' points of view • **Time Management:** Budgeting time for reading and note-taking
Written Language	• Fine Motor skills: pencil grip, letter formation, use of space on a page • Writing fluency: speed and accuracy	• **Initiation:** Ability to start assignments. • **Planning:** Pre-writing (web or outline); Using words to guide a reader to a logical conclusion • **Shifting:** Thinking flexibly and anticipating a reader's reaction to your words • **Monitoring:** Assessing and editing your work • **Working Memory:** Keeping in mind writing skills.
Independent Studying, Homework, and Long-term Projects	• Using a planner • Bringing home needed materials • Having a set study time and place	• **Planning:** Envisioning short- and long-term tasks • **Shifting:** Transitioning from school to home, and completing your work independently • **Monitoring:** Assessing and editing your work • **Organizing Materials:** Gathering items for school, home, and play
Test-taking	• Knowing what to study • Ability to recall relevant information	• **Organizing Materials:** Making sure you have easy access to study guides and materials • **Planning:** Setting time to study before a test and managing time during a test • **Shifting:** Applying your knowledge to different contexts and integrating different ideas • **Monitoring:** Assessing and editing your work before turning it in

What Does the Executive Functioning Program Do, and How Do I Start?

As noted, the Executive Functioning Program increases your ability to plan, start, and finish work on your own. It exercises the neurological activity that creates Executive Functioning by helping you identify your aims, build thinking skills, and practice good organizational strategies. In brief, this program establishes your academic autonomy as you get better at determining your goals and applying the habits that let you attain them.

Strengthening any Executive Functioning skill first requires developing self-knowledge and self-control. These powers give you the most important talent you'll ever master: **self-regulation**, or the ability to know and manage your feelings. Once people become aware of their thought processes (especially their emotions), they're better able to control their actions and focus on what's important to them.

To polish that talent, you first need what's called *metacognition*—a technical word that means "thinking about thinking." When you use metacognition, you come to understand how you personally think and learn. Those metacognition skills will soon let you prompt yourself to get through the steps in a project. They will let you ask yourself questions about what you need to do, identify those steps, confront, and overcome challenges in doing them, and complete them to achieve your goal.

Program Components
- Self-assessment of academic skills
- Setting your academic and personal goals
- Organizing your backpack

Student Workbook

- Equipping your study space at home
- Using a planner to track daily, weekly, and long-term assignments
- Accurately estimating how long homework will take
- Scheduling time for homework, study, and other activities
- Breaking down long-term projects into daily tasks
- Active reading and study skills
- Taking useful notes on lectures and texts
- Test preparation and test-taking strategies
- Presentation preparation and performance strategies
- Tracking your progress and setting your new goals

How the Program Works

As noted, the program starts by increasing your awareness of your unique learning style and based on that lets you set and learn how to meet your goals.

The first step is to explore your view of your challenges and strengths relating to schoolwork. Understanding the areas you have mastered and those that need to be developed allows you to personalize your EF program.

Each unit of the workbook includes **creative exercises** and **checklists** to use as executive functioning tools. To access new strategies, students must become aware of their own feelings and impulses to allow them to regulate their thoughts, emotions, and actions. The creative exercises help students get in touch with their feelings so that they can take control over them. The checklists are good tools to help students breakdown and stay on track. Checklists provide external structure for skills students have not yet mastered.

Student Workbook

The Flow of the Program

- After this **INTRODUCTION AND RATIONALE** unit, the workbook guides you step by step as you build your Executive Functioning skills and make them habitual. These steps will become your self-prompts to keep yourself independently on track: STOP AND IMAGINE; THINK AND PLAN; DO AND REVIEW; CHECK AND TURN IN. The program trains you in each of these self-prompts—the habits you want to own.

- Unit 1, **Take the Executive Functioning Quiz and Set Goals**, sets you on your path to success. The Executive Functioning Quiz will help you understand the areas you have mastered and the areas you need to build. This knowledge of your abilities will allow you to set goals to guide you.

- Unit 2, **STOP AND IMAGINE,** shows the power of simply *pausing* to get ready for work before you even begin. That's because it's crucial to become aware of your feelings and impulses surrounding schoolwork, and to learn to regulate your thoughts, emotions, and actions so you can concentrate on your aims. Once you've learned to STOP AND IMAGINE *what* you need to do, it will be much easier to figure out exactly *how* you're going to do it. Taking time to understand the task, to organize your mind and feelings, and to clear out and restock your backpack and desk sets you up for success. This step allows you to visualize precisely what you want to achieve.

- Once you've stopped to consider your task, you can plan how to do it. Unit 3, **THINK AND PLAN,** outlines how to use a planner to manage your time and energy. You'll make and follow clear checklists to achieve each of your goals. This unit gives you concrete strategies to develop organizational habits, along with useful short-term (or working) memory tips.

- Unit 4, **DO AND REVIEW**, details the action steps you'll use to follow your plan. It also guides your preparation for, and performance on, tests and presentations. But as you may have noticed, while tests and presentations are important, this program focuses first on skills for completing schoolwork and studying on your own. The reason for prioritizing homework habits is that doing assignments both requires and sharpens the same abilities you'll later use for tests and presentations:

  - Breaking down complex projects into manageable, logically ordered tasks
  - Correctly estimating how long tasks will take
  - Starting, stopping, and changing activities when needed
  - Using short-term working memory

- Unit 5, **CHECK AND TURN IN**, gives you concrete ways to make sure your finished work matches your goal. It provides strategies for monitoring your products' quality and your time. Using these tips and techniques until they're automatic lets you master organized, efficient completion of your tasks.

- A bonus sixth unit, **REASSESS**, lets you assess how much you've learned from this program, and what new goals you'd like to take on.

It is never too late to improve old skills and to create new ones. You'll find that practicing new executive functioning skills helps you work quickly and efficiently.

Quiz and Goal Setting

UNIT ONE

EF QUESTIONNAIRE AND GOAL SETTING

Set Up a Successful Executive Functioning Plan

People with Executive Functioning difficulties do best when tasks have been broken down into manageable, ordered steps. Generally, students who aren't organized tend to become overwhelmed by the prospect of the task ahead. If you've ever had this feeling, it's probably what stops you from being able to start and finish your work. Learning how to look at a task, break it down into doable, efficient steps, list them, and follow them one by one grows your Executive Functioning skills—as well as your independence, confidence, and enjoyment of learning.

Understanding your current skills will allow you to set realistic goals. Take the Executive Functioning Questionnaire to see which Executive Functioning tasks you already do well and which ones you can strengthen to help you in school.

Take the online questionnaire: kandmcenter.com/executive-functioning-quiz. When you are done write your scores in the score sheet so you can see how you did

Quiz and Goal Setting

Exercise: Your Executive Functioning Scores

Record your scores in each area. How well do they match what you see as your strengths and weaknesses? Don't worry about the actual numbers; it's the difference between your higher-score areas and your lower-score areas that shows your strengths and challenges.

Executive Functioning Questionnaire Scores

Your Scores	EF Skill	Interpretation of Low Scores
	Working Memory: The ability to remember information for immediate use.	You may find it difficult to remember a series of directions or have a hard time solving problems that involve more than one step
	Organizing Materials: The ability to organize objects in work, play, and storage areas.	You struggle to supply and straighten your workspace, living area, and backpack so you have everything you need.
	Planning: The ability to manage tasks by setting goals and developing steps to achieve the goals.	You may read instructions over and over but not know what steps you need to complete to finish it on time
	Emotional Control: The ability to regulate emotional responses to stress.	You may have trouble getting over a disappointment, or find that you get frustrated often, which can get in the way of achieving your goals.
	Initiation: The ability to get started on tasks without many prompts and cues.	You may sit down to do your work, but not know what to do first.
	Time Management: Allotting appropriate time for each task.	You may be spending too much or too little time on tasks
	Monitoring: The ability to judge the quantity and quality of one's work based on expected standards.	You might miss cues from others about whether you are performing or behaving as expected.
	Shifting: The ability to transition from one activity to another or a way of thinking about or doing something in another way.	It may be hard for you to make transitions to different tasks or activities.

Quiz and Goal Setting

Student Interview

Now that you know your executive functioning strengths and weaknesses, take a moment to review your academic skills at school.

Have someone ask you the interview questions and record your answers. Use this interview as a chance to reflect on yourself as a learner and to consider your strengths and weaknesses. This reflection will help you set goals to work on as you go through the Executive Functioning Workbook.

Student Interview

Take a minute to answer questions below and record your answers like a reporter. Use this review as a chance to reflect on yourself as a learner and to consider your strengths and weaknesses. This reflection will help you set goals to work on as you go through the Executive Functioning Workbook.

ENGLISH
Do you like English?
Do you consider it a strength or a weakness?
How is reading? <ul><li>What are your favorite books?</li><li>Which books have you disliked?</li><li>Do you read what is assigned?</li><li>Does it take you a long time to get through your reading assignment?</li><li>Do you usually understand the meaning of the literature?</li><li>Do you take notes in your book in your book or mark key passages as you read?</li></ul>
How is your writing? <ul><li>Do you like to write?</li><li>Do you type your assignments?</li><li>Does writing take you a long time?</li><li>Do you find it easy or hard to decide what to write about?</li><li>Do you make webs or outlines before writing?</li><li>Do you write a rough draft? Do you make revisions before or after the paper is due?</li><li>What comments do you usually get from your teacher?</li></ul>

Quiz and Goal Setting

MATH
How's math? Do you consider yourself a good math student?
What has been your easiest math class? Your hardest?
Is your homework easy or hard? Do you turn it in on time?
Do you take notes in class to help you with your homework later?
How do you prepare for tests?   • How do you do on tests?
What kind of errors do you make?   • Conceptual?   • Careless?
What comments do you usually get from your teacher?
HISTORY
Do you consider yourself a good history student?
Does the reading seem hard?
How good are your note-taking skills?   • in class   • form texts
How do you do on exams?   • What comments do you usually get from your teacher?   • Do you prefer short answer, multiple choice, or easy tests?
How do you study for tests?   • Do you go to review sessions, study with friends or a tutor?   • Study your notes and make flashcards?

SCIENCE
How's science?   • Do you consider yourself a good science student?
What's your favorite part of science?   • What was your favorite science class?   • Your least favorite?
Is your homework easy or hard? Do you turn it in on time?
Do you take notes in class to help you with your homework later?
How good are your note-taking skills?   • In class   • from texts
How do you do on exams?   • What comments do you usually get from your teacher?   • Do you prefer short answer, multiple choice, or essay tests?
How do you study for tests?   • Do you go to review sessions?   • Study with friends or a tutor?   • Make flashcards?

Quiz and Goal Setting

Goal Setting

Now that you've filled out the Executive Functioning Questionnaire and done some thinking about yourself as a learner, you can set specific goals for yourself. Keeping in mind your strengths and challenges and your answers to the questions above, what do you think are the top three things you'd like to improve?

Remember to make them reasonable and set a goal you think you can reach. For example, if you have trouble keeping your binder organized, a reasonable goal might be:

- "For 10 minutes every school night, I'll file all the loose papers in my binder, including its front pocket."

Also, keep your goals measurable so you can monitor how well you're achieving them. For example, it's hard to measure "I'll manage my time better." But if you rewrite your goal as, "I'll be on time to all my appointments this week and use the time management checklist to plan each day," you'll be able to measure your progress towards that goal easily. For another example, it's hard to measure "I'll do my homework." But if you rewrite your goal as "I'll use the Daily Homework Checklist each night to plan out my homework and check it off when I'm finished," you can measure your progress towards that goal over time.

Quiz and Goal Setting

Exercise: Your Executive Functioning Scores

My Goals:

1.
2.
3.
4.
5.
6.

Quiz and Goal Setting

Time to Reflect ....

- What will my life look like when I achieve my goals?

- What do I need to do to make my life easier right now?

- Can I write a reasonable and measurable goal about this? (If not, you may want to rewrite it.)

- What is going to motivate me to make these changes?

Now that you have set doable and measurable goals, you are ready to dive deeper into the Executive Functioning skills you're using when you STOP AND IMAGINE your material and space. Keep in mind the results of your Executive Functioning Questionnaire, which showed you the strengths you already have that will help you STOP AND IMAGINE, and which skills you might want to build.

UNIT TWO

STOP AND IMAGINE

What Do I Need To Do?

Now that you understand your abilities and have set goals, it is time to start building your executive functioning skills. The first step to building Executive Functioning skills is to STOP AND IMAGINE your thoughts about what you want to do.

It might seem odd but spending the time to get organized saves you time. Pausing to collect your thoughts before jumping into an assignment allows you to plan efficiently to get work done quickly. Organizing materials in your backpack and work areas also saves time as you can quickly find what you need. Take a moment to consider the Executive Functioning skills needed to STOP AND IMAGINE.

EXECUTIVE FUNCTIONING SKILLS TO HELP YOU STOP AND IMAGINE:

> **STOP AND IMAGINE**
> **Executive Functioning Skills**

INHIBITION	Stopping off-task behavior
SHIFTING	Moving from one idea or activity to another
EMOTIONAL CONTROL	Regulating stress and distractibility
PLANNING	Setting goals and the steps to accomplish them
ORGANIZING MATERIALS	Organizing objects for work, play and storage

STOP AND IMAGINE

The following skills build executive functioning skills needed to STOP AND IMAGINE thoughts and materials. Look back at your Executive Functioning Quiz results and see if any of these areas you need to develop. A skill building exercise is presented after each executive functioning skill. Select the skills you want to strengthen and try the exercises.

Once you have identified the skills you want to build and practiced with the exercise, there are checklists to help you STOP AND IMAGINE your materials.

Inhibition: The ability to stop off-task actions when you need to.

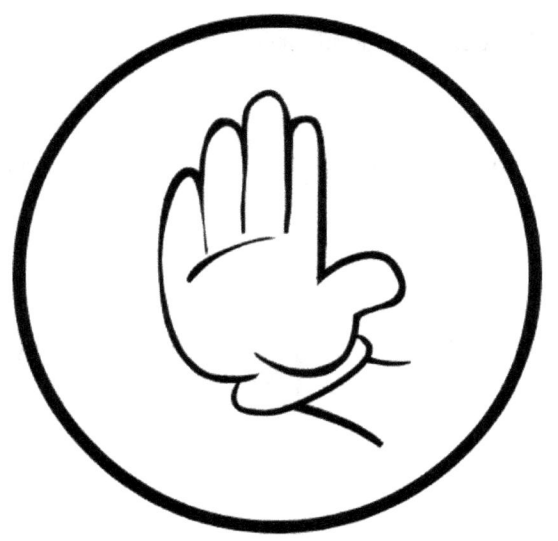

People who have difficulty inhibiting behaviors might:

- Blurt out comments in the middle of class
- Lose focus in class from minor distractions, like someone walking in or a noise from outside
- Have difficulty following rules
- Often say things they later regret
- "Borrow" items without asking
- Lie because it seems easier and safer than telling the truth

The first step to inhibiting your behavior—stopping off-task actions when you need to—is to become aware of the value of stopping to reflect before you say or do something, or to "look before you leap." Of course, acquiring the habit of stopping yourself can be very difficult when your mind is running fast, or you're just not used to holding off on words and actions. That's why this program helps you exercise that power, so you can more easily inhibit your automatic responses—so you can stop yourself for a bit before you speak or act.

Help yourself take a minute to STOP and clear your mind before you start working. Train your mind to take control over your thoughts and actions rather than letting your mind control you.

STOP AND IMAGINE

Exercise: Clear Your Mind

Materials

Paper; chalk/ pastels/ crayons/ colored pencils/ markers. You can also use the online resource: mindfuldraw.com or use an actual Buddha Board to watch the scribble disappear and clear from the virtual or actual screen.

Instructions

Give the prompt: *"Let's clear out your mind by scribbling. Grab some crayons, markers or pens and some paper. Take just a minute and draw any kind of scribble. Let your mind be free."*

- After the student has finished, say, *"You can show me your scribble or keep it just for you. Either way, now your mind is clear and ready to work!"*

Shifting: Moving from one idea or activity to another

Signs of difficulty shifting include:

- Repeatedly asking, "What's happening next?" during a transition, even if it's been explained multiple times
- Discomfort before, during, or after transitions
- Relying on external structure (ordered steps and deadlines) to do good work

The first step to powering up your shifting skill is to become aware of the need to switch your thoughts and energies from what you've been doing to the next task. Shifting is the core of flexible thinking—the ability to let go of one idea or feeling and to consider another idea or feeling. When you're thinking flexibly—"out of the box"—you're shifting, which is a crucial Executive Functioning skill.

Whenever you get stuck and realize you're not heading toward your goal, take a moment to scan your thoughts and see if you can shift them—to come up with another way to think about the task. Use your shifting skill to become a flexible thinker.

Need help shifting? Here are some questions you can ask yourself whenever you feel stuck in one idea or activity:

- How am I doing?
- Am I heading toward my goal?
- Am I on the right track?
- Am I spending the right amount of time on this?

STOP AND IMAGINE

- Do I understand the directions? If I don't, what do I need to do?
- What strategies am I using?
- Is there a better strategy I could use?
- How will I know when I'm done?

Exercise: Flex Your Brain

Materials

Optical illusions copied from a book (such as *The Ultimate Book of Optical illusions by Al Secke* or *Amazing optical illusions by illusionWorks*) or an online site (such as illusions.org. or kids.niehs.nih.gov/games/riddles/illusions)

Instructions

Give the prompt: *"Let's play some mind shifting games. Each of these pictures is an optical illusion. There is more than one way to look at the picture. When you are able to shift what you focus on in the picture you will see something different!"*

- Have the student look at and solve the illusions by finding multiple images within one picture.
- Ask the student to note what s/he saw immediately.
- Then prompt the student to close their eyes and look again focusing on a different part of the picture.
- If it's hard to see an alternate image:
  - Cover up parts of the picture and invite the student to trace the outline of the image with a finger.
  - Hold or place the picture at a greater distance. Sometimes a different perspective can help!
  - Ask the student to try squinting until s/he sees the alternate image.
  - Print 2 copies of one image and have the student color them in 2 different ways.

STOP AND IMAGINE

Exercise: Inhibition with *Stroop*

YELLOW	YELLOW	GREEN	BLUE	RED
GREEN	YELLOW	BLUE	RED	RED
BLUE	YELLOW	GREEN	YELLOW	RED

Materials

Go to Memozor.com/other-memory-games/words-memory-games/stroop-effect-game or any Stroop Test.

Instructions

- Follow the prompt or direction online. The student will practice switching his/her attention between competing aspects of a stimulus.
- Mark the number of errors and discuss why it can be hard to stop the impulse to just read the word and remember the rules. Taking a moment to shift from the immediate impulse to the rule requires inhibition. This game is a fun way to build skills.

Exercise: Draw Infinity

Materials

This exercise can be done with or without materials. Students can draw with markers or crayons on paper, with chalk on the ground, or simply in the air with a finger or on the ground with a foot.

Instructions

Give the prompt: *"Drawing the infinity sign helps your brain alternate between its left and its right side by crossing what's called the midline. Crossing the midline helps information flow more freely so you can understand it in many ways. Whenever you feel stuck, drawing the Infinity sign can help you get unstuck."*

- Ask the student to draw infinity signs in the air or on paper, with her/his foot on the floor, or to walk it on the ground–any preferred way.

Exercise: How Many Ways

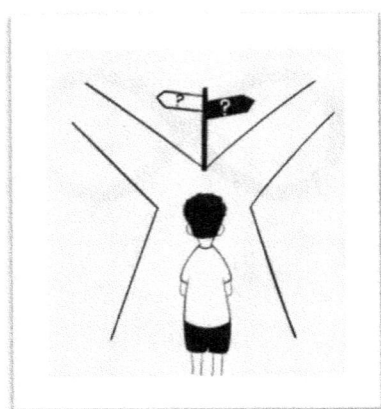

Materials

Print out a street-view map from Google Maps or any other map, and mark a Point A and a Point B.

Instructions

Give the prompt: *"There can be many ways to solve a problem, such as how to get from one place to another. Let's see how many different paths you can find from point A to point B on this map"*

- Ask the student to estimate the shortest distance between point A and point B.
- Invite her/him to find alternative routes between the same locations.
- Count how many routes the student can find between the two locations.
- Ask the student, *"Which route do you think is the shortest in length?"*
- Ask the student, *"Which route do you think is the quickest to travel?"*

Emotional Control: Regulating stress and distractibility

Strengths in emotional control include appropriately expressing emotions, whether negative or positive. The key word is *appropriately*. For example, rude people may be annoying, but expressing your annoyance with an angry outburst of mean comments is inappropriate. Besides hurting another person's feelings, it doesn't get the job done. Another example is loud rejoicing when you or your friend's team wins over a rival without considering the other team's disappointment. A final, worst example of inappropriate emotional expression is physically hurting someone or even damaging an item when you're angry.

Check how strong your emotional control is when:

- You receive a bad grade.
- You lose out on a spot on the team or in a performance.
- Your team loses.
- Your team wins.

What are some ways you react when you lose control of your emotions? Do you...

- use your body inappropriately rather than words to express emotions.
- have a meltdown.
- say things without thinking.

Exercise: Feeling Wheel

Materials

Drawing materials, clay, puppets or cards. You can also use online resources:

- onlinepuppets.org
- onlinesandtray.com
- oaklandertraining.org/projective-cards

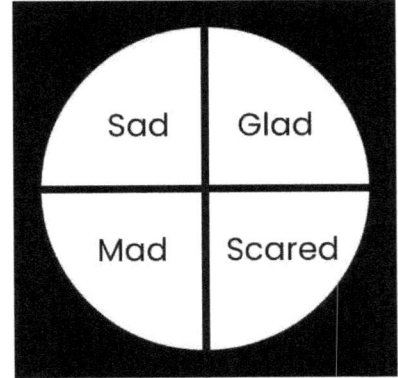

Instructions

Give the prompt: *"You are going to use your imagination to think about different feelings, what it feels like to you when you are sad, mad, glad or scared. Right now, you'll just be thinking about your feelings, not really experiencing them. But thinking about your feelings can help you notice what they feel like and help you recognize them in a real situation. Being able to identify and think about your feelings will let you take control of your emotions. We are now going to practice identifying your emotions."*

Leave time for the student to think and respond, then continue:

- *"Close your eyes if you want to, take a breath, and try to feel one of the emotions on the Feeling Wheel—sad, mad, glad or scared."*

- *"Which did you pick?"*

- *"Where do you feel it in your body? What does it feel like?"*
- *"Draw a picture or pick an object, card or puppet that reminds you of that feeling."*
- *"Now, do the same with each of the other feelings."*

Leaving time for reflection and responses, guide the student to integrate thinking with feeling.

- *"Now, think of an area of difficulty for you."*
- *"Pick a card or puppet, make a clay objects, or draw a picture that goes with your struggle."*
- *"Close your eyes if you want to, take a breath, and try to feel the emotion that goes with this situation."*
- *"Where do you feel it in your body? What's that feeling like?"*
- *"Express that feeling by describing it in words, turning it into a sound. or drawing it."*
- *"Now, you can integrate what you're thinking with you're feeling."*
- *"What internal and external supports can you find to address this feeling?"*
- *"What do you think those supports will say and do?"*
- *"How will those supporting words and actions change what you're feeling?"*

STOP AND IMAGINE

Exercise: Feeling Pyramid

Materials

10 small pieces of paper or Post-Its; pencil

Instructions

Give the prompt: *"On each piece of paper or Post-It, write down one thing you're frustrated or angry about."*

- Have the student organize the papers or Post-Its into a pyramid, with the most frustrating/angering one at the top and the least frustrating/angering ones at the base.
- Ask, *"Why did you put them in that order?"*
- Ask *"Who can help you?"*

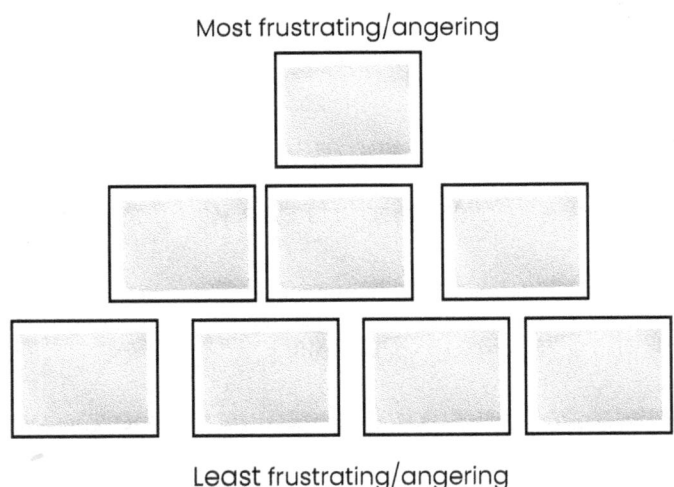

Monitoring: Judging the quality and pace of work

Signs of weak monitoring include:

- Running out of time on assignments
- Taking all night to complete homework
- Stopping a task before you finished it
- Turning in incomplete homework

Questions to help you monitor yourself:

- What do I need to do?
- Am I doing what I planned to do?
- Is this taking the amount of time I expected?
- Am I following the directions correctly?
- Did I complete this task correctly?

STOP AND IMAGINE

Organizing Materials: Organizing objects for work, play and storage

Signs that you struggle with organizing materials:

- You constantly tell others, "I know where everything is, it's just my system."
- Your backpack has layers of items, some of which would surprise or horrify you.
- It's hard for you to find what you need in your backpack, your room, or your desk.
- You would have difficulty telling someone else how to find something you left at home or at school.
- You frequently forget something at home or at school.
- You arrive at school or home without all the materials you need.

Do you recognize any of these signs? If so, learning to organize your materials can save you time and energy.

Asking yourself these questions will help you organize materials:

- Where's the best place to store this so I can easily find it again?
- What do I need for the task I am doing?
- Where does this belong?

Exercise: Rate Your Backpack and Workspace

How neat is Your Backpack?

Take a deep breath, look at your backpack, and rate how organized it is.

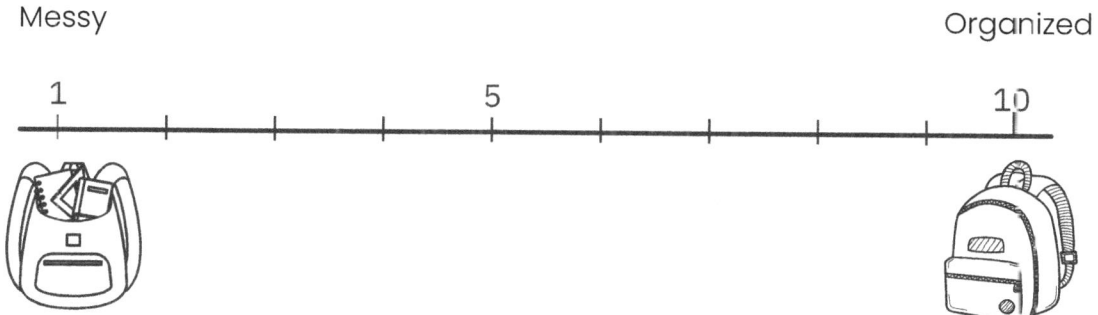

Now, look at your workspace and rate how organized it is.

How neat is Your Workspace?

Now steel yourself to look at your workspace and rate how organized it is.

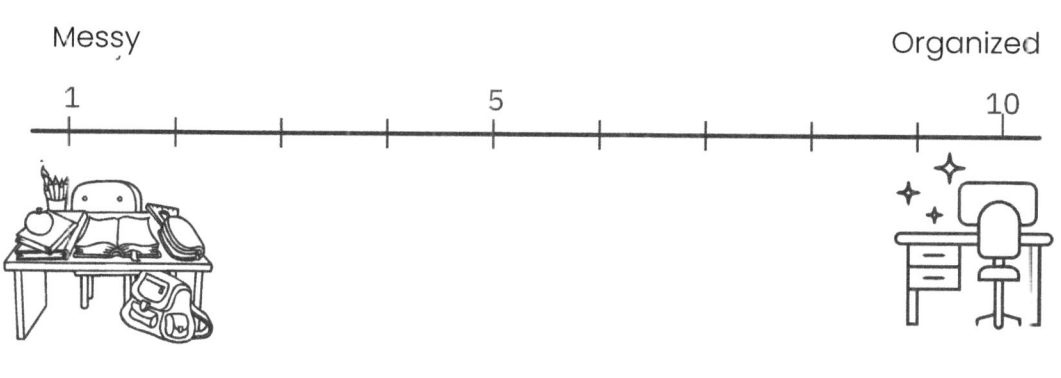

STOP AND IMAGINE

Using your STOP AND IMAGINE skills

Ever notice how knowing where everything is in a space makes it look bigger and more open? Well, organizing your workspaces can also open your mind! Imagine getting back from school and being able to find everything you need from your backpack quickly and easily, leaving you time to think about the assignments instead of stressing over materials you can't locate! Learning the basics of organizing your personal items will help you keep your backpack—and your thoughts—in order and open to new ideas.

Organize your Backpack

An organized backpack keeps your school life and your personal life going smoothly. It has all the correct items to bring to and from school daily so you can complete homework, study for tests, eat a nice lunch and snacks, and be ready for your day.

Check your backpack twice a day:
- Before you leave home in the morning, and
- Before you leave school in the afternoon.

Check in the morning to make sure you have all the materials—learning and personal—you'll need in school. Then check in the afternoon before you leave to make sure you have everything you need to complete your homework that night and have a good next day at school.

Checklist: Morning Checklist

Before you leave home in the morning, ask yourself:

DO I HAVE?.....

TO BRING TO SCHOOL	YES, I HAVE IT	NO, I NEED TO GET IT
Planner		
Completed homework- in my binder for that subject, or in a designated homework folder		
Books, binders, or folders for each subject that I have that day		
Pens and pencils to take notes		
Paper		
Clothing for warmth and after-school activities		
Ask myself: Am I forgetting anything?		
Other materials:		

STOP AND IMAGINE

Checklist: Afternoon Checklist

Before you leave school in the afternoon, ask yourself:

DO I HAVE?.....

TO BRING HOME	YES, I HAVE IT	NO, I NEED TO GET IT
Planner filled out so I know my assignments		
Binders		
All the books I need to complete homework and assignments		
Folders		
Handouts from teachers telling me details about my assignments and upcoming tests		
Slips or notes for parents		
Clothing -- hat, sweater, jacket		
Gym clothes		
Ask myself: Am I forgetting anything?		
Other materials		

Each day, when you get home from school, **take everything out of your backpack!** Take out papers and file them in the correct place, throw away old lunches, put gym clothes in the laundry, and put that extra calculator you've been looking for where it belongs.

Once you get in the habit of cleaning your backpack daily, it should take just a few minutes. This quick checklist will remind you what to look for:

Checklist: Quick Daily Backpack Checklist

TO DO	DONE
Clean out backpack and toss out garbage.	○
Put pencils and pens in container or zipped compartment.	○
File all papers in my binders/folders.	○
Make sure homework is where it belongs.	○
Put parent handout materials in binder or folder.	○

STOP AND IMAGINE

Checklist: Weekly Backpack Checklist

Check off each task you completed each day of the week. Doing this lets you track how well you're building the STOP AND IMAGINE habit.

Check off each task you have completed each day.

TO BRING TO SCHOOL	M	T	W	TH	F	S/S
Completed homework -- in my binder for that subject, or in a designated homework folder						
Books, binders/folders/computer/iPad for each subject that I have that day						
Pens and Pencils to take notes						
Paper						
Planner						
Clothing for warmth and after-school activities						
Other						
Ask myself: Am I forgetting anything?						

STOP AND IMAGINE

TO BRING HOME	M	T	W	TH	F	S/S
Binders						
Books						
Folders						
Planner filled out so I know my assignments						
Handouts from teachers telling me details about my assignments and upcoming tests						
Slips or notes for Parents						
Clothing-- hat, sweater, jacket						
Gym clothes						
Other						
Ask myself: Am I forgetting anything?						

STOP AND IMAGINE

Checklist: Backpack Organization

BACKPACK ORGANIZATION	M	T	W	TH	F	S/S
Cleaned out backpack and tossed out garbage						
Pencils and pens in container or zipped compartment						
Assignment section or planner						
All papers filed in my binders/folders						
Designated sections for my homework-- either a separate folder, or in a binder with dividers						
Parent handout section or folder						
Ask myself: Am I forgetting anything?						

Checklist: Nightly Sign Off

	M	T	W	TH	F	S/S
STUDENT						
PARENT						

Organize your Study Space

Along with an organized backpack, a tidy and well-stocked workplace lets you quickly find the materials you need to complete your projects so you can put your energy into thinking, not searching.

Take a moment to visualize the place you usually work.

If you don't have a consistent place, now's the time to pick one, since using one workspace helps you keep all your materials together so it's easier to stay organized.

My choice of a workspace:

Keep your study space filled with needed supplies, arranged neatly enough to find, so you can quickly get ahold of materials for completing your homework.

If you have more than one favorite space—maybe you're sometimes in a different home, or just like some variety—you can easily create a portable materials holder for everything you need. The key step is to make sure you have everything you need at your fingertips so you can spend your energy thinking, not stressing and hunting! Now you are ready to evaluate your workspace in terms of what it has and what it needs:

STOP AND IMAGINE

Checklist: Workspace Needs

> Evaluate your workspace in terms of what it has and what it needs:

Physical Space	Have	Need
A specific space to work		
A good work surface and chair		
Area to file papers and organize books (cupboard, shelf, desk, of file cabinet)		
Good lighting		
Quiet		
Freedom from interruptions		

What did you find? Does your workspace let you store what you need to get your work done? If not, consider another place that might be better. Use the checklist again to make sure the new place can and does hold what you need.

STOP AND IMAGINE

Checklist: Workspace Materials Worksheet

MATERIALS	HAVE	NEED
Homework assignment and materials		
Planner and monthly calendar		
Timer		
Contact information of at least 3 reliable classmates (to call it you forgot to write down any homework.)		
Extra pencils and pens		
Pencil Sharpener		
Highlighters and colored pencils		
Post it notes or different sizes and colors		
White-Out		
Paper, lined and graph		
Stapler		
Ruler		
Paper clips		
Erasers		
Scissors		
Tape		
Glue or paste		
Wastebasket		
3-hole punch		
Index cards: lined or unlined, white or colored		

©2023 KandMCenter.com

STOP AND IMAGINE

MATERIALS (continued)	HAVE	NEED
Folders for reports		
Extra binders		
Dividers		
Small accordion file		
Calculator		
Computer		
Is there anything else that you know you will need?		

STOP AND IMAGINE

UNIT THREE

THINK AND PLAN

How Will I Achieve My Goal?

THINK AND PLAN

Once you've identified your goal, it's time to plan how to achieve it. Planning breaks a project into manageable, logically ordered tasks, creating a roadmap for you to follow toward your goal.

Knowing how much time you must have to complete a task and how long the task takes is the first step. A **calendar** helps you plan your time for schoolwork and other activities, while a **planner** can help you keep track of each step you need to do. **Checklists** are also helpful tools to plan and monitor your work.

EXECUTIVE FUNCTIONING SKILLS TO HELP YOU THINK AND PLAN:

THINK AND PLAN
Executive Functioning Skills

WORKING MEMORY	Remembering information for immediate use
PLANNING	Setting goals and the steps to accomplish them
TIME MANAGEMENT	Allotting appropriate time for each task
SHIFTING	Moving from one idea or activity to another
MONITORING	Judging the quality and pace of work

THINK AND PLAN

Working Memory: Remembering information for immediate use

Signs of Working Memory difficulties include:

- Frequently walking out the door without the things you need
- Forgetting what happened at the beginning of a passage once you reach the end
- Getting lost in multi-step directions, even if you understand the basic task
- Losing track of your ideas while writing them up
- Losing your train of thought in conversation

Strategies to build Working Memory Skills

- Organize information in meaningful ways.
- Chunk the information into shorter steps.
- Connect new information with previously learned information.
- Preview new concepts so you know what to expect.
- Build strategies to help analyze, prioritize, and execute specific steps in each assignment.
- Think through your responses and take your time.
- Break down tasks and create a checklist and then follow the order checking work along the way.
- Rehearse new information to help encode it.
- Visualize what you are going to do before you begin a task.
- Use reminders (which can be set on devices such as the iPhone) to help remind you to stay on task.

Exercise: Alphabet Memory Stretch

Materials

2 or more players

Instructions

Give the Directions:

- *"This game will strengthen your memory skills. We're going to think of- and remember- items that begin with each letter of the alphabet in order starting with A."*
- *"The first player names something that starts with A, and the second player repeats the A item and adds something that starts with B."*
- *"The next player says the A and B items, and names something that starts with C. Each player in turn repeats all the items previously named in order and adds a new item that starts with the next letter in the alphabet."*
- *"The game lasts until one player forgets an item- or you reach the letter Z!"*

A   B   C   D

THINK AND PLAN

Exercise: The Connection Game

(for 2 or more players)

No materials needed

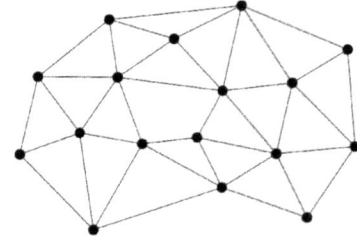

Instructions

Give the prompt: *"Working Memory is when you can remember and work with information. We are going to help build your working memory skills by making connections. Making connections and creating images can help you store information in a meaningful way so you can retrieve it later. This game will strengthen your association skills. We're going to find items that are connected in some way. The connection can be the color, shape, use, category or any other logical connection you can think of."*

- **Step 1:** *"The first player names something that can be seen in the room, then the second player names something in the room that has some connection the first object".*
- **Step 2:** *"Each player in turn names an object that is connected in some way to the last object named".*
- **Step 3:** *"The game continues around the group until no more connections can be made".*

See how many connections you can make!

Shifting: Moving from one idea or activity to another

Signs of difficulty shifting include:

- Being stuck on one task without being able to move on to other work you must also do
- Choosing a research topic that is so broad you won't have the time to write it up
- Allotting a task the same amount of time on your planner every day even though you've seen it always takes longer

REMEMBER: Whenever you realize you've gotten stuck and are not heading toward your goal, take a moment to scan your thoughts and see if you can shift, or change, them to think about the problem or task differently. Use your shifting skills to become a flexible thinker.

Need help shifting? Here are some questions you can ask yourself whenever you become stuck in any activity:

- How am I doing?
- Am I heading toward my goal?
- How should I proceed?
- Am I spending the right amount of time on this?
- What do I need to do if I get stuck?
- What do I need to do if I don't understand?
- How will I know when I'm done?
- What strategies am I using?
- Is there a better strategy I could use?

THINK AND PLAN

Exercise: The Scribble Drawing

NOTE: Scribble Drawing is a fun way to build the ability to shift using many learning modalities: gross motor skills, fine motor skills, visualization, working memory and following directions, as well as expressive language.

Materials

1 piece of paper as tall and wide as the student, 2 different-colored markers. See a demonstration at https://www.kandmcenter.com/demonstrations.

Instructions

- **Give the prompt:** *"I'd like you to stand up with one marker, with the cap on, in your stronger hand. Now, imagine a piece of paper that's exactly the height and the width of your body. The paper goes from your head to your feet and from one side of you to the other side. You're going to draw a quick scribble on this imaginary piece of paper. I'm going to give*

THINK AND PLAN

you 10 seconds, which I will count out, and you draw your imaginary scribble in the air with me."

- "Ready?" Count to 10 slowly while the student scribbles in the air.
- "Now go to your real piece of paper and make that design from top to bottom on your real piece of paper with your marker, now with the cap off. Be quick! whatever your scribble in the air was, that's what you draw on your paper, from top to bottom."
- Let the student draw the scribble.
- "Now put that first marker aside. Look at your scribble and pick the second marker and use it to make something out of your scribble - It can be a shape, design or anything."
- Give the student about 5 minutes to add to the scribble creation. Then invite the student to share what they made.

THINK AND PLAN

Monitoring: Judging the quality and pace of work

Here's a reminder of some signs of weak monitoring:

- Frequently running out of time on assignments
- Taking all night to complete homework
- Stopping a task before you have finished it
- Turning in incomplete homework

Questions to help you monitor:

- What do I need to do?
- Am I doing what I planned to do?
- Is this taking the amount of time I expected?
- Am I following the directions correctly?
- Did I complete this task correctly?

Exercise: Questions to Help You Monitor Your Progress

> Questions to guide you through a task

STOP	THINK	DO	CHECK
• What should I be doing right now? • Do I need to stop what I am doing to start this new task?	• What is the teacher asking me to do? • What do I visualize the final product looking like? • Do I have a checklist that I can use to help me plan each step? • What materials will I need? • Who can I ask for help if I need it?	• What steps do I need to complete in order to finish the project? • What should I do first? • What step comes next? • Did I write all of the steps down in the order I need to complete them? • How much time will each step take? • Did I remember to fit in breaks? • When should I complete each step? (Write it down to hold yourself accountable) • Will I have enough time to finish?	• What step am I working on? • Am I marking the progress I should be making? • Am I staying on task? • Am I marking off each step as I complete it? • Is my plan working? If not, how can I improve it? • Does this look like what I thought it would?

THINK AND PLAN

Time Management: Allotting the correct amount of time for what you want to do

Signs of Time Management difficulties include:

- Having a project you thought would take only an hour, putting it off until the last minute, and realizing it was going to take a lot longer than you thought
- Frequently running out of time when taking tests or doing homework
- Frequently being late for school or appointments

Underestimating how long activities take causes huge frustration. But using the tools in this unit can really help prevent that aggravation. When planning your time you can use the STOP, THINK, DO, and CHECK prompts to help you, along with the checklists in this unit.

Sometimes it may feel like there just isn't enough time in the day to finish everything you have to do, and that's an awful feeling. The first step in combatting that bad feeling is pinning down all the different activities that fill your day, and then deciding how long each one takes. That way, you can map out your schedule to see how much time you REALLY have each day for homework, projects, and studying.

These are the steps you'll go through each time you start a new task. The more times you walk through these steps, the more automatic the process becomes. Asking yourself questions as you move through a task will help you take control of your brain—you just need to know which questions to ask yourself.

Take a moment to consider what it would feel like to have an Internal Timekeeper that helps you know how long things take to do and how much time you have left.

THINK AND PLAN

Exercise: How Accurate is My Sense of Time

How Accurate is Your Sense of Time

Estimate how long each of the following activities takes you, then time yourself doing each one to see how long it really takes.

ACTIVITY	HOW LONG DO I THINK IT TAKES?	HOW LONG DID IT REALLY TAKE?	WHAT WAS THE DIFFERENCE?
Brushing Your Teeth			
Eating Breakfast			
Getting Dressed and Ready for School			
Eating Dinner			

THINK AND PLAN

Let's move on to another exercise that will show you how much of your day is already full of scheduled activities such as school, sports, and music lessons and how much of your day is left to complete homework, studying, and projects.

Use the chart on page 116 to fill in how long each activity takes. Then, transfer the information to a weekly chart to keep track of exactly when you'll complete each activity. If you're not sure how long an activity takes, use a timer when you're doing it to get a more accurate idea. For instance, you might think it takes you just 20 minutes to get ready for school, but once you time it, you may find out it takes closer to an hour, or only 10 minutes.

THINK AND PLAN

Exercise: Internal Timekeepers

Materials
Piece of paper, crayons/markers/pens/pencils

Instructions

Give the prompt: *"Take moment to consider what it would feel like to have an internal timekeeper that helps you know how long things take to do and how much time you have left. We all have an internal timekeeper who manages our "Internal clock" and measures our time. In this activity you get to imagine the internal timekeeper you have now, then imagine an ideal one, and see how they might work together to help you."*

Step 1

- **Imagine It:** *"Let's start by imagining what your current internal timekeeper looks like-the one you have now."*
- **Make It:** *"Draw a picture of your current internal Timekeeper. It can be just shapes, colors, lines, or objects."* Give the student 1 minute to draw.
- **Own It:** *"Look at your picture and give it a short descriptive title.*

Step 2

- **Imagine It:** *"Now, imagine what your ideal internal Timekeeper would look like"*
- **Make It:** *"Draw a picture of your Ideal internal Timekeeper. "Give the student 1 minute to draw."*
- **Own It:** *"Look at your picture and give it a short descriptive title.*

Step 3

- **Imagine It:** *"Next, imagine what the bridge from your current Internal Timekeeper to your ideal internal Timekeeper look like."*
- **Make It:** *"Draw a picture of the bridge."* Give the student 2 minutes to draw.
- **Own It:** *"Look at your picture and give it a short descriptive title."*
- **Extend It:** *"Now, that you can imagine what it would like to have a good sense of time, consider how long your daily activities are taking you now."*

THINK AND PLAN

Exercise: What Activities Fill Up Your Day?

Daily Activities

DAILY ACTIVITIES	Mon	Tue	Wed	Thu	Fri	Sat	Sun
Getting ready for school							
Getting to school							
Hours in school							
Extracurricular activities (sports, club, music, tutoring)							
Getting home from school							
Homework/ Studying							
Dinner							
Relaxation reading TV/ Video games							
Socializing with friends/ family							
Last-minute studying							
Getting ready for bed							
Sleeping							
Other							
TOTAL:							

** Remember, there are 24 hours in a day, so each day should equal exactly 24 hours. **

Exercise: Daily Schedule

Now that you have figured out how long each activity takes, you need to determine when you are going to complete each one.

- Mark off on your schedule when you wake up and how much time it takes you to get ready for school.
- Enter in the time that you are at school each day.
- Mark off all extracurricular activities - sports, clubs, tutoring, art classes, music etc. that you do after school. Don't forget to include weekend activities as well.
- Also mark off the time you eat dinner each night as well as the time you need to be in bed.
- Now that all of your activities are marked on your schedule, highlight all of your free time in yellow.

	Mon	Tue	Wed	Thu	Fri	Sat	Sun
6:30 a.m.							
7:00							
7:30							
8:00							
1st Period							
2nd Period							
3rd Period							
4th Period							
5th Period							
6th Period							
7th Period							
3:00 p.m.							
3:30							
4:00							
4:30							
5:00							
5:30							
6:00							
6:30							
7:00							
7:30							
8:00							
8:30							
9:00							
9:30							
10:00							

THINK AND PLAN

Or, if you do not have set class periods each day,
you can use this schedule instead to fill in all of your activities.

	Mon	Tue	Wed	Thu	Fir	Sat	Sun
6:30 a.m.							
7:00							
7:30							
8:00							
7:00							
7:30							
8:00							
8:30							
9:30							
10:00							
10:30							
11:00							
11:30							
12:00							
12:30							
1:00							
1:30							
2:00							
2:30							
3:00							
3:30							
4:00							
4:30							
5:00							
5:30							
6:00							
6:30							
7:00							
7:30							
8:00							
8:30							

©2023 KandMCenter.com

Exercise: Questions About Your Schedule

Questions to ask after filling in daily schedule

- Is this the amount of free time I thought I had each day?
- How much time do I have each day to complete schoolwork?

Monday	
Tuesday	
Wednesday	
Thursday	
Friday	

- Are there any days that I have more time than others?
- Can I use this day to get ahead on any studying / projects?
- Are they any days that I don't have much time for homework?
- Are there any assignments that I do the night before to help make this day more manageable?

THINK AND PLAN

Planning: Setting goals and the steps to accomplish them

Once you have stopped, shifted your attention to the task and managed any frustration about the task, you are ready plan your actions.

Signs of poor planning skills:
- Trouble starting or completing long-term assignments
- Forgetting to bring home necessary books, binders, or other materials
- Writing papers or stories that have hard-to-follow plots
- Starting a project without all the necessary materials
- Turning in assignments that didn't follow the teacher's guidelines

Building planning skills starts with understanding what your goal is, and then making a roadmap to get there. Planning questions include:
- What steps do I need to complete to finish this project?
- What step should I do first?
- Did I write all the steps down in the order I need to complete them?
- How much time will each step take?
- Did I remember to fit in breaks?
- When should I complete each step?

THINK AND PLAN

Planners are a valuable tool. They help you track what you need to do and when it is due. Many schools have online portals where teachers note homework, tests, and grades. However, these portals are not always up to date and don't always cover your workload. Keeping your own planner lets you see current assignments and tests in each class, as well as other projects you may have. Plus, it feels great to check off an item in your planner when it's done and turned in!

Once you have a planner, you need to use it—it can't help you if it stays blank in your backpack. A planner also helps you track all your activities. You may think you'll remember everything, such as when a teacher gives you a special project, or when your sports event is, but by the time you get home you may have forgotten an important detail. This guide will show you if you're using your planner effectively and, if not, how you can make it help you even more.

THINK AND PLAN

Exercise: Questions to Help You Plan

STOP / ORGANIZE QUESTIONS

- What am I being asked to do?
- What do I visualize the final product looking like?
- Do I have a checklist that I can use to help me plan each step?
- What materials will I need?
- Whom can I ask for help if I need it?
- Where is the best place to do this project?

THINK / PLAN QUESTIONS

- What steps do I need to do to finish this project?
- What should I do first?
- Did I write all the steps down in the order I need to complete them?
- How much time will each step take?
- Did I remember to fit in breaks?
- When should I complete each step?

Using your THINK AND PLAN skills

Using a Planner

Exercise: Picking a Planner

It is best to use the planner that your school provides if that's an option. If your school does not provide a planner, then there are some important points to consider when selecting one.

Does the planner have...

- ○ ... a daily calendar with enough space to write down all assignments by subject?
- ○ ... enough space to write all assignments neatly?
- ○ ... an area for important phone numbers?
- ○ ... a full-year calendar?
- ○ ... a monthly calendar?

THINK AND PLAN

Checklist: How to Use a Planner

DO YOU USE YOUR PLANNER WELL?

Check off each item that you add to your planner

- ◯ All homework assignments, including pages and problem numbers
- ◯ Due dates for projects and papers
- ◯ Test and quiz dates
- ◯ Extracurricular activities, such as clubs, sports games, and student council
- ◯ After school activities, like tutoring, piano and art classes
- ◯ Study group and review sessions
- ◯ Meetings with teachers

THINK AND PLAN

Exercise: When to Use Your Planner

Now, let's discuss when you need to check your planner during the day.

Check off the times you use your planner	
○ Before leaving for school in the morning...	to make sure you have everything you need for the day
○ At the beginning of each class...	to see if you have anything to turn in
○ At the end of class...	to see if there are any new assignments written on the board that you need to write in your planner
○ Before you leave school in the afternoon...	to make sure you have all the materials you will need to plan and complete your homework
○ Before you go to bed...	to make sure you did all homework put materials back in your backpack for the next day

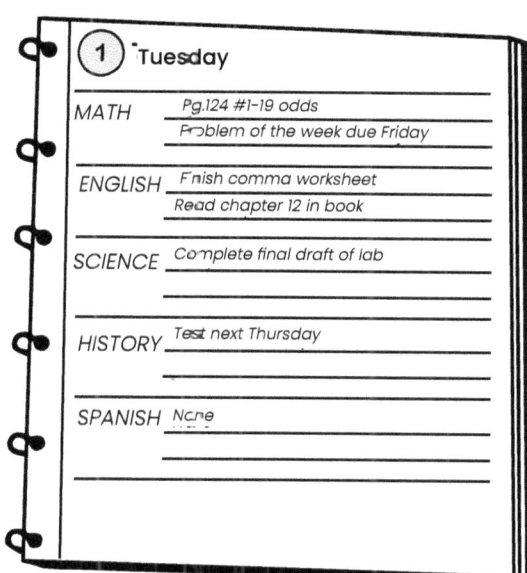

Using your planner will help you remember the work that gets assigned throughout the day.

THINK AND PLAN

Checklist: How to Use a Planner

DO YOU USE YOUR PLANNER WELL?

Check off each item that you add to your planner

- ○ All homework assignments, including pages and problem numbers
- ○ Due dates for projects and papers
- ○ Test and quiz dates
- ○ Extracurricular activities, such as clubs, sports games and student council
- ○ After school activities, like tutoring, piano and art classes
- ○ Study group and review sessions
- ○ Meetings with teachers

Long-Term Planning

Long-term assignments such as essays, book reports, or science projects, can be broken down into small, manageable, logically ordered steps.

- First, put the due date on your monthly calendar.
- Then figure out how much time you have from today to the due date.
- Break the assignment in action steps you need to do to complete it.
- Now you know how many days you have, and you can start planning when you'll finish each step.
- Write the steps in your planner.

Use the STOP, THINK, DO, CHECK prompts and checklists to help you complete long-term projects.

THINK AND PLAN

Steps for Planning Essays, Projects, and Reports

Remember to use STOP, THINK, PLAN, DO prompts as you work.

Remember to use STOP, THINK, DO, CHECK questions to ask questions as you work.

STOP	THINK	DO	CHECK
• Read the directions. • Make sure you understand the assignment.	• When is it due? • What steps do you need to complete in order to finish the assignment? • What do you need to do first? • Fill in your checklist. • Write in the steps on your monthly calendar. • Decide when you will complete each step and how long it will take.	• Start working • Follow your schedule. • Make sure to check off each step as you complete it.	• What step am I working on? • Am I making the progress I should be making? • Am I staying on task? • Am I marking off each step as I complete it? • Is my plan working? if not, how can I improve it? • Does this look like what I thought it would?

Example *Steps for Long-Term Planning*

Long-term Planner

Assignment/Test: History Research Paper on Civil War.
Due date: In 2 1/2 weeks (Assigned: Sept. 6th Due: Sept. 22nd)

WHAT DO I NEED TO GET DONE?	HOW LONG WILL IT TAKE?	WHEN WILL I DO IT?	CHECK WHEN DONE!
STEP 1: Read assignment and pick topic	1 hr.	Tues. 9/6	○
STEP 2: Do research	3 hr.	Sat. 9/10	○
STEP 3: Read material and take notes	5 hr.	Sun. 9/11 - 2 hrs. Mon. 9/12 - 1 hrs. Tues. 9/13 - 1 hrs. Wed. 9/14 - 1 hrs.	○ ○ ○ ○ ○
STEP 4: Organize material and do outline	3 hr.	Sat. 9/17	○
STEP 5: Write draft	3 hr.	Sun. 9/18	○
STEP 6: Edit draft	1 hr.	Mon. 9/19	○
STEP 7: Have parent or teacher review		Tues. 9/20	○
STEP 8: Make revisions	1 hr.	Wed. 9/21	○
STEP 9: Turn it in!		Thurs. 9/22	○

THINK AND PLAN

Example Monthly Calendar

Assignment/Test: History Research Paper on Civil War

Due date: Assigned: Sept. 6th; Due: Sept. 22nd (in 2½ weeks)

Monthly Calendar

Assignment/Test: History Research Paper on Civil War.
Due date: In 2 1/2 weeks (Assigned: Sept. 6th Due: Sept. 22nd)

SEPTEMBER

SUNDAY	MONDAY	TUESDAY	WEDNESDAY	THURSDAY	FRIDAY	SATURDAY
				1	2	3
4	5	6 Read assignment and pick topic	7	8	9	10 Do research
11 Read materials and take notes	12 Read materials and take notes	13 Read materials and take notes	14 Read materials and take notes	15	16	17 Organize material and make outline
18 Write draft	19 Edit draft	20 Have parent to teacher review	21 Make revisions	22 Turn it in!	23	24
25	26	27	28	29	30	

Checklist: Long-Term Planning

Assignment/Test: _____

Due date: _____

WHAT DO I NEED TO GET DONE?	HOW LONG WILL IT TAKE?	WHEN WILL I DO IT?	CHECK WHEN DONE!
STEP 1:			○
STEP 2:			○
STEP 3:			○
STEP 4:			○
STEP 5:			○
STEP 6:			○
STEP 7:			○
STEP 8:			○
STEP 9:			○

THINK AND PLAN

Exercise: Monthly Calendar

Transfer each step onto your monthly calendar. Hang your monthly calendar in an easily visible location.

Long-Term Assignment Calendar

Transfer each step onto your monthly calendar.
Hang your monthly calendar in a visible location.

Assignment/Test: _____

Due date: _____

Fill in the months and dates on the calendar before you enter your steps.

SUNDAY	MONDAY	TUESDAY	WEDNESDAY	THURSDAY	FRIDAY	SATURDAY

Calendar and Planner Apps

These are some of the apps that offer different programs helping with a variety of tasks. Check them out with a teacher, parent, or coach.

Note: New programs are constantly being created, so once you determine the features you're looking for, you can search for a program that best meets your needs.

THINK AND PLAN

Calendar and Planner Apps

App	Description	Where
Microsoft To Do	Daily planner, task manager, reminders, attachments, sharing, and more.	Free on all devices
Google Calendar	Allows for sync option for events and schedules from a Google account with other apps, events, and schedules.	Free on all devices
Google Tasks	Set due dates and reminders. Can create multiple lists for different Google accounts and add emails to task for collaboration.	Free on all devices
Trello	Collaborative app for meetings, projects, events and goal setting.	Free, with paid upgrades available, on all devices
My Study Life-School Planner	Track tasks, store assignments and exams in the cloud, accessible anywhere. Manage classes with timetables and notifications.	Free on all devices
Todoist	Manage and share tasks, sub-tasks, sub-projects, recurring tasks, notifications, different priorities and more.	Free, with paid upgrades available, on all devices
Time Timer	Turns phone, computer or smartwatch screen into a fun, bold, circle timer.	Free on all devices

THINK AND PLAN

UNIT FOUR

DO AND REVIEW

What Is My First Step?

DO AND REVIEW

Sometimes the hardest part of a job is knowing where to start. The checklists you created and the planner you filled out in Unit 3: PLAN will now guide you through the DO stage of your work. This DO unit outlines the action steps to help you follow your plan.

EXECUTIVE FUNCTIONING SKILLS TO HELP YOU DO AND REVIEW:

DO AND REVIEW
Executive Functioning Skills

INITIATION	Starting work
WORKING MEMORY	Remembering information for immediate use
MONITORING	Judging the quality and pace of work
EMOTIONAL CONTROL	Regulating stress and distractibility

Consider for a moment the Executive Functioning skills you're using when you do a task. Look back at the results of your Executive Functioning Quiz to find the strengths you have that can help you do your work and which skills you might want to build.

DO AND REVIEW

Initiation: Starting Work

You learned how to plan your work in Unit 3, now it is time to use the Executive Functioning skill of Initiation—the ability to start work. Doing and completing work begins with starting the task. Often people who have trouble starting their work are seen as procrastinators. The following exercise will help you gain an awareness of the side of you that procrastinates, The Procrastinator and the part of you that can get started, The Initiator.

Signs of Initiation difficulties include:

- Staring at an assignment without reading the directions
- Repeatedly getting more supplies or snacks or going to the bathroom instead of starting work
- Spending hours on homework, but getting only a little bit done

DO AND REVIEW

Following the STOP AND IMAGINE, THINK AND PLAN, DO AND REVIEW, CHECK AND TURN IN prompts will help you break down tasks into manageable steps, and get started. Asking yourself questions as you work can help guide you. Here are examples of questions to ask yourself as you move through a project:

STOP / ORGANIZE QUESTIONS	THINK / PLAN QUESTIONS
<ul><li>What am I being asked to do?</li><li>What do I visualize the final product looking like?</li><li>Do I have a checklist that I can use to help me plan each step?</li><li>What materials will I need?</li><li>Whom can I ask for help if I need it?</li><li>Where is the best place to do this project?</li></ul>	<ul><li>What steps do I need to complete to finish the project?</li><li>What should I do first?</li><li>Did I write all the steps down in the order I need to complete them?</li><li>How much time will each step take?</li><li>Did I remember to fit in breaks?</li><li>When should I complete each step?</li></ul>

DO AND REVIEW

Exercise: Turn the Procrastinator into the Initiator

Materials

Drawing materials, clay, puppets, or cards. You can also use online resources:

- onlinepuppets.org
- onlinesandtray.com
- oaklandertraining.org/projective-cards

Instructions

Give the prompt: "Let's imagine that there's an Internal Timekeeper who manages your 'internal clock' and helps you measure your time. Sometimes the Timekeeper may be called 'The Procrastinator,' and sometimes the Timekeeper may be called 'The Initiator.' Now imagine what happens when The Procrastinator is in charge and what happens when The Initiator is in charge. Then you can figure out how to build a bridge to keep the more helpful one in charge."

Step 1

- **Imagine it:** *"Imagine a scene in which you have trouble starting a task and you procrastinate."* Give the student 30 seconds to imagine the scene.
- **Make it:** *"Draw, choose a card, or make a clay object that represents you when you have trouble starting a task."* Give the student a few minutes to depict themselves when procrastinating.

DO AND REVIEW

- **Be it:** *"Speak as though you're The Procrastinator."* Let the student speak or make sounds.
- **Own it:** *"How and when does being The Procrastinator fit for you in your life?"* Allow the student a moment to respond. Now tell the student, "We're going to do this game again, but this time envision yourself beginning work right away

Step 2

- **Imagine it:** *"Imagine a scene in which you start working right away—you initiate it."* Give the student 30 seconds to imagine the scene.
- **Make it:** *"Draw, choose a card, or make a clay object that represents you as The Initiator."* Give the student a few minutes to depict her/himself when initiating.
- **Be it:** *"Speak as though you're The Initiator."* Let the student speak or make sounds.
- **Own it:** *"How and when does being The Initiator fit for you in your life?"*

Step 3

- **Imagine it:** *"Imagine a bridge from The Procrastinator to The Initiator.*
- **Make it:** *"Draw, choose a card, or make a clay object that represents the bridge."* Give the student a few minutes to depict her/himself creating a bridge.
- **Be it:** *"Speak as though you're the bridge."* Let the student speak or make sounds.
- **Own it:** *"How and when does being bridge fit for you in your life?"*

DO AND REVIEW

Emotional Control: Regulating stress and distractibility

Some people have trouble starting tasks while others have difficulty completing them. If it's hard for you to finish work, the step by-step system will help you get through each part. If you find yourself stuck or wanting to give up, STOP for a moment. Take a deep breath, sip some water, wiggle your toes, roll your shoulders back—any of these natural pauses will help regulate your feelings. Ask yourself some questions to help you focus on your goals.

Questions to help you regain your focus:
- What's my goal?
- Why did I pick or accept that goal?
- What am I feeling right now?
- How do I want to feel?
- How do I get from here to there?

Tips for Test Anxiety
- Best remedy is preparation (see planning, time management, and study skills).
- Use meditation, breath work, apps such as Calm, Headspace, Heartmath.

Tips for Frustration

- Strengthen flexible thinking/ability to "shift" perspective.
- Make an anger/frustration list, and process how you deal with the items.
- Maintain perspective when you are frustrated by comparing how important the problem is to the size of your reaction.
- Create a checklist of what you would like from the situation and how you think you can get there.

Exercise: Get Back on Task

Quick Reflection to Get Back on Task	
What I want	The steps to get what I want

The Feeling Wheel was introduced in Unit 2. It is a value tool to use whenever you want to understand and take control of your emotions.

DO AND REVIEW

Exercise: Feeling Wheel

Materials

Drawing materials, clay, puppets or cards. You can also use online resources:

- onlinepuppets.org
- onlinesandtray.com
- oaklandertraining.org/projective-cards

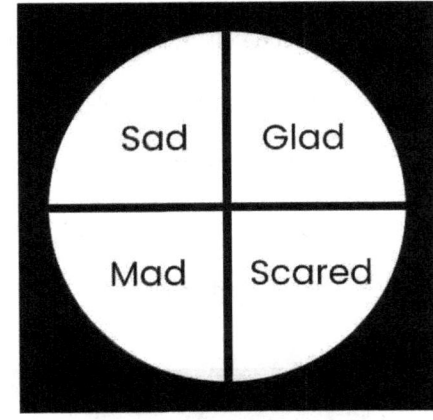

Instructions

Give the prompt: "You are going to use your imagination to think about different feelings, what it feels like to you when you are sad, mad, glad or scared. Right now, you'll just be thinking about your feelings, not really experiencing them. But thinking about your feelings can help you notice what they feel like and help you recognize them in a real situation. Being able to identify and think about your feelings will let you take control of your emotions. We are now going to practice identifying your emotions."

Leave time for the student to think and respond, then continue:

- "Close your eyes if you want to, take a breath, and try to feel one of the emotions on the Feeling Wheel-sad, mad, glad or scared."
- "Which did you pick?"

- "Where do you feel it in your body? What does it feel like?"
- "Draw a picture or pick an object, card or puppet that reminds you of that feeling."
- "Now, do the same with each of the other feelings."

Leaving time for reflection and responses, guide the student to integrate thinking with feeling.

- "Now, think of an area of difficulty for you."
- "Pick a card or puppet make a clay object, or draw a picture that goes with your feeling."
- "Close your eyes if you want to, take a breath, and try to feel the emotion that goes with this situation."
- "Where do you feel it in your body? What's that feeling like?"
- "Express that feeling by describing it in words, turning it into a sound, or drawing it."
- "Now, you can integrate what you're thinking with you're feeling."
- "What internal and external supports can you find to address this feeling?"
- "What do you think those supports will say and do?"
- "How will those supporting words and actions change what you're feeling?"

DO AND REVIEW

Exercise: The Gatekeeper

Optional Materials

Paper and chalk / pastels / crayons / colored pencils / markers

Instructions

Give the prompt: *"Did you know that you can control the flow of information in your mind? When your mind is clear information flows easily. However, when you get upset, or anxious, your mind tries to protect you and shuts down. When your mind shuts down it is hard for you to think. You can open your brain flow by imagining a gatekeeper who controls your thinking. You can tell the gatekeeper that you are fine, and it is safe to let your ideas flow, so you can think easily again."*

- **Imagine it:** *"Imagine that your gatekeeper is sitting right in front of your brain controlling all the information going in and out. What does your gatekeeper look like?"* Give the student time to imagine the gatekeeper.
- **Make it /Share it:** *"Can you draw or describe what your gatekeeper looks like?"* Give the student a few minutes to share their image.
- **Be it:** *"Speak as though you're the gatekeeper. Tell me what your job is."* Let the student speak.
- **Own it:** *"How and when does working with the gatekeeper fit in your life?"* Allow the student a moment to respond.

DO AND REVIEW

Monitoring: Judging the quality and pace of your work

Monitoring was discussed in Unit 2 and Unit 3. Practicing it is the best way to make yourself an independent learner and getting good at it is the best proof that you've become an independent learner. That's because checking whether you're on task and making adjustments when you realize you're off task is the core of managing your own education. Use your metacognitive skills—thinking about your own thinking—to monitor your plan and your performance of it by asking yourself:

- How am I doing?
- Am I following the directions?
- What do I need to do next?
- Does this match what I planned?
- Am I getting enough done in the time I am spending?
- Do I need to ask for help?

Monitoring helps you overcome the constant distractions from technology and the many demands on you throughout the day as a student, athlete, child, or sibling. Another great way to manage your focus on what you need to get done is to immerse yourself in an external environment with as few distractions as possible. You've started doing that by keeping your backpack neat and your study space well-supplied. Now that you've learned about organization in Unit 2 and about time management and planning in Unit 3, you're finally ready to apply those skills to the fine art of doing homework.

Did you find that you overestimate or underestimate how long homework will take you each night? Did it seem that there's just not enough time to get everything done?

DO AND REVIEW

Since you've become a better estimator of how long assignments and other activities actually take you, you can better plan how long you need to complete homework each night.

Use the Daily Homework Planner on the next page to help see how accurate your estimates are as you complete your homework.

Exercise: Daily Homework Planner

You will find directions for using this planner on the next page.

SUBJECT	TASK	ESTIMATED TIME NEEDED	REAL TIME NEEDED	DIFFERENCE

DO AND REVIEW

How to use the Daily Homework Planner

Use Your Daily Homework Planner

STOP AND IMAGINE

- Look at your planner
- Review your short-term and long-term assignments. Write both types of assignments under "tasks."
- If you don't know the homework in one of your classes, call a friend to get the information.

THINK AND PLAN

- Identity what's due tomorrow. Plan to do those assignments first.
- Assess which are hardest for you. Plan to do the hardest ones first and save the easiest ones for later.
- Number the assignments in the order you plan to do them.
- Estimate the amount of time each assignment will take and write it down.
  - Add up how much time all your work will take.
    - Write down when you will take breaks and add that to your total time.
    - Calculate when you will be done with your work based on your starting time, break time and estimated work time. Do you have enough time?

DO AND COMPLETE

- Set the timer when you start each assignment and stop it when you're finished.
- On your chart, record the actual time you spent.
- Note any differences – how close was your estimated time to the time you actually spent?

CHECK AND TURN IN

- Check off each assignment as soon as you have finished it.
- Pack each assignment in its place in your backpack, or make sure you saved it on your computer.
- Turn it in to your teacher.

Time to Reflect

- What did you notice about your estimates of time needed per assignment?
- Were you accurate, or do you need to start giving yourself more time or less time to complete homework each night?
- Planning your time to complete both long-term and short-term assignments will make them easier to finish, and you won't find yourself always getting things done at the last minute.

DO AND REVIEW

Exercise: Nightly Homework Plan

Once you start becoming a good estimator of how long assignments will take, you can start to use this homework planner to schedule the correct amount of time to complete each assignment. Some students find it helps to have a schedule right in front of them so they can see if they are on track with their estimates.

DO AND REVIEW

TIME	Homework TO DO Today	DONE
3:00 p.m.		
3:30		
4:00		
4:30		
5:00		
5:30		
6:00		
6:30		
7:00		
7:30		
8:00		
8:30		
9:00		
9:30		
10:00		
10:30 p.m.		

DO AND REVIEW

Using your skills

Use the STOP and THINK skills you learned in Units 2 and 3 to organize the steps for the task before you start working.

STOP and **IMAGINE**, then **THINK** and **PLAN**:
- What will your work look like when it is complete?
- Check to make sure you have all the materials you need.
- Create a checklist to track each step you'll do to complete the assignment.
- Prioritize the tasks into what needs to be done first, second, third.
- Estimate the time each step will take.
- Add up your estimated amounts of time per step to find how long the entire assignment will take and to plan your time.

Now you're ready for DO AND REVIEW:

- Start with the highest-priority task: the hardest one among the soonest due.
- Set the timer when you start each item on your list and stop it when you finish.
- On your chart, record the actual time each task took.
- What was the difference?
- Were you close?
- Check off each task when it's done and start the next task.

DO AND REVIEW

Follow these tips to maintain your efficiency and performance:

DURING CLASS
- Put your phone out of sight and out of reach (in your backpack/desk drawer).
- Stay engaged, raise your hand, be involved in discussion.
- Take out only what you need immediately (book, folder, iPad–with only the apps you need running).
- If you're near people who distract you, ask if you can move!

AT HOME
- Frequently check your schedule and work plan—try to avoid being surprised by something you forgot.
- Make sure you have a consistent, quiet workspace that minimizes outside distractions (TV, foot traffic into the kitchen).
- Have everything you need at your workspace, so you don't need to get up repeatedly.
- Dedicate pure work time, but schedule frequent breaks to avoid drifting.

Using your DO AND REVIEW Skills

Active Reading

Active reading—picturing and questioning what you're reading in a textbook, novel, or handout—deploys your imagination and recall, which helps you understand and retain what you read. There are specific strategies, tailored to different types of books, which you can use before, during, and after reading to ensure you capture and keep the material.

DO AND REVIEW

Tools for Active Reading

Before Reading: Planning

- Ask: "What am I supposed to be learning?
- Think: What do I already know?
- Preview: Skim, look at pictures/ captions, timelines.
    - Look at chapter titles: What do these tell me about the book?
- Predict: "What will I learn?
- Prepare: Decide on the note-taking format you will use.

During Reading

- Take notes or annotate using post-its or colored highlighters in the book to underline/ highlight key information.
- Who are the important characters?
- What is the most important event in each chapter?
- Think, "Can I briefly summarize what I just read?"
- Make a list of characters and describe each one.
- Make connections: "Have I ever felt that way before?" or "Have I read/seen something similar to this before?"
- Highlight new vocabulary words.
- Make a vocabulary list, and find the definitions.

After Reading

- Review the vocabulary terms.
- Reread your chapter summary list - can you give a verbal summary of the book?
- What was the conflict, or problem?
- How did they resolve the conflict?
- Think, "What did I like most about this book? What did I not like?"
- Reflect on your process while reading.

DO AND REVIEW

Checklist: Character List

Use this handout to help you keep track of characters as you read.

CHARACTER'S NAME	DESCRIPTION	WHY ARE THEY IMPORTANT IN THE STORY?

©2023 KandMCenter.com

159

DO AND REVIEW

Chapter Summaries

- Jot down major events in each chapter to help you remember what happened.
- Textbooks used in science, social studies, or other fact-heavy classes require different active reading strategies. One proven method to help you understand and remember texts is known as SQ3R.

Exercise: SQ3R (Survey, Question, Read, Recite, Review)

SURVEY:	• Title, headings, and subheadings • Captions under pictures, charts, graphs or maps • Review questions or study guides • Introductory and concluding paragraphs • Summary
QUESTION WHILE YOU ARE SURVEYING	• Turn the title, headings and/or subheadings into questions • Read questions at the end of the chapters or after each subheading • Ask: "What did my instructor say about this chapter or subject?" • Ask: "What do I already know about this subject?"
READ:	• Look for answers to your questions • Slow down for complex information • Pay attention to visual cues in the book: charts, graphs, diagrams, and words in bold
RECITE:	• Restate the question, then give your answer. Underline or highlight the portion of the text where you found the answer.
REVIEW:	• Go back and reread the highlighted sections • Use the key words in the margin to remember the main ideas • Make flashcards for any information you need to remember • Test and retest yourself using your notes and flashcards

DO AND REVIEW

Exercise: Chapter Summary

Jot down several important events in a chapter to help you remember what happens in each chapter.

CHAPTER _____:
-
-
-

CHAPTER _____:
-
-
-

CHAPTER _____:
-
-
-

CHAPTER _____:
-
-
-

CHAPTER _____:
-
-
-

CHAPTER _____:
-
-
-

Exercise: Active Reading Review

After you read, reflect on what helped you comprehend and retain the material, and on what areas you want to improve. Use this checklist to help you reflect on your reading:

DID I...

- READ THE ASSIGNED PAGES? ☐

- USE ACTIVE READING STRATEGIES TO HELP ME UNDERSTAND? ☐
  - Preview the text ☐
  - Take notes/ use the active reading tools ☐
  - Use the active reading bookmark ☐

- UNDERSTAND WHAT I READ? ☐

DO AND REVIEW

Active reading is a major part of being an engaged, effective, independent learner. Taking good notes is another. Using active reading skills and effective note-taking strategies will help you to remember the information you read or hear.

Using good note-taking skills helps you learn new information and access it when you need it. Remember to use your STOP, THINK, DO, CHECK questions from Unit 2.

DO AND REVIEW

Note-Taking Prompts

Remember to use STOP, THINK, DO, CHECK questions to ask questions as you work.

STOP	THINK	DO	CHECK
• Get ready to take notes	• What unit are you studying? • What topic does the reading or lecture cover? • What do you already know about this topic? • What is the best note-taking format to use? • What materials do I need? (book, highlighter, etc.) • What is the best note-taking format to use?	• Start reading, highlighting and taking notes	• What step am I working on? • Am I making the progress I should be making? • Am I staying on task?

Note-Taking Tips

Note-Taking Tips

- Use a notebook, binder, or computer.
- Write the subject, date, and topic on the top of the page.
- Separate the main idea from the details.
- Use as few words as possible with bullet points and abbreviations.
- Write down key words or phrases to remember.
- Use your own words when taking notes from a book, avoid copying directly from the book.
- Underline or highlight important information.
- Go over your notes - make sure you understand what you've written.
- Write any questions you have and edit your notes to be clear.
- Summarize the most important information.

Format Notes

Divide your Page

- Fold your paper lengthwise into two unequal sections: the left 1/3 of the page width and the right 2/3 of the page width, or on a screen, make a table with similar columns.
- Then, write or type the main ideas from the lecture on the left side of the page and the supporting details on the right.
- Leave enough space between main ideas so you can fit the details parallel to the main point they back up.

DO AND REVIEW

Divide your page or computer document into main ideas and supporting details.

❶ First, fold your paper into a 1/3 section on the left and a 2/3 section on the right.

❷ Then, write the main ideas from the lecture on the left side of the page and the supporting details on the right.

Main Idea	Supporting Details
	•
	•
	•
Main Idea	Supporting Details
	•
	•
	•
Main Idea	Supporting Details
	•
	•
	•

Summary of what is covered on this page of notes

DO AND REVIEW

An outline also separates the main idea from the supporting details.

Example:

Richard Meier

Richard Meier is a world-renowned American architect who completed a majority of his most famous work in the 1970s and 1980s. He was born in Newark, New Jersey on October 12, 1934. Meier received his degree in architecture form Cornell University in 1957, at which point he traveled to Europe in hopes of learning from the then-prominent Mid-Century Modern designers. After two years, Meier returned to New York where he worked for several architecture firms until 1963 when he began working with four other prominent American architects-Peter Eisenman, Charles Gwathmey, Michael Graves, and Jhon Hejduk. The five men became known as the "New York Five" and were celebrated for their innovative, playful and unique designs.

Although Meier's work is considered to be in the Post-Modern style, his largest architectural influences were Mid-Century Modern designers such as LeCorbusier and Mies Van Der Robe. When designing his homes and buildings, Meier focuses largely on space, from and light and the manipulation of each to emphasize a structure's surroundings. In fact, Meier's methods and philosophy regarding the use of form to create light and shadow to define space continues to inspire and influence architects today.

Upon seeing Richard Meier's work, it is easy to see the basic themes of space, from and light play out. It is also apparent as you view his work chronologically that, while his earlier work seemed to have some of the more boxy, purist influence typical of the Mid-Century Modern style, Meier eventually seems to become a bit more playful in his designs. While Meier has a bountiful portfolio of exceptional work, perhaps his three most famous buildings include The Getty Center in Los Angeles. The Barcelona Museum of Contemporary Art, and The Atheneum in New Harmony, Indiana.

---

1 Main idea
a) Supporting detail
b) Supporting detail
c) Supporting detail

2 Main idea
a) Supporting detail
b) Supporting detail
c) Supporting detail

3 Main idea
a) Supporting detail
b) Supporting detail
c) Supporting detail

→

1 Richard Meier-world famous American Architect
a) 1957 - graduated Cornell University
b) 1963 - began work with the "New York Five"
c) Most famous work done in the 1970s - 1980s

2 The focus of Meier's building and home design:
a) Space
b) Form
c) Light

3 3 most famous works:
a) The Getty Center in Los Angeles
b) The Barcelona Museum of Contemporary Art
c) The Atheneum in New Harmony, Indiana

DO AND REVIEW

In classes where you are learning about events in chronological order, a timeline can be used.

- Write the starting date on the far left side of the line.
- Plan the dates you will be adding and mark them on the line.
- Add specific facts until the time sequence is complete.

1776: Declaration of Independence

1812: War with Great Britain

1861-1865: American Civil War

While you can easily make a timeline while reading a textbook, it's a bit harder to do it while listening to a lecture. If the lecturer presents a lot of dates and events, you might take out a blank sheet of paper to make a timeline—or you could have a copy of a blank timeline ready for you to fill in when you hear dates.

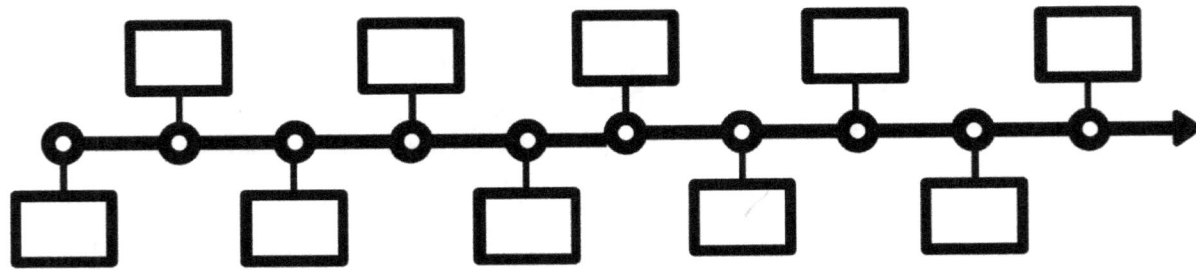

You can use a graphic organizer program like Mindomo to create graphic organizers on the computer. Simply drag and drop bubbles to organize and categorize concepts and ideas. Establish connections with links to connect ideas. The structure is automatically generated for you when you use Arrange or when you view your diagram as an outline.

Note-taking Apps

These are some of the apps that offer different programs helping with taking notes. Check them out with a teacher, parent, or coach.

Note: New programs are constantly being created, so once you determine the features you're looking for, you can search for a program that best meets your needs.

DO AND REVIEW

Note-Taking Apps

App	Description	Where
Notability	Mark up imported documents, record/ playback audio, create schedules, sync to Dropbox or Google Drive.	Free, on all devices, with some in-app purchases
Notion	Write, plan and organize in one place. Drag and drop anything.	Free, on all devices, for personal users.
ScanMarker	Scan physical text into a digital document. It can also translate and read aloud text.	Software free, on all devices. Marker is $109
Temi	Speech-to-text app. Upload any audio or video file, then download the transcript.	$0.25/ minute
GoodNotes	Digital notebook for document organization and editing. It can import, sync, draw and erase.	$7.99, one-time purchase. iPhone, iPad, Mac iOS only.
Mindomo	Create mind maps and easily edit them. Helps Organize ideas.	Free version or $5.50/ month, single user cloud + Mobile + Desktop

Studying for tests

At last, it's time to start applying everything you've learned about Executive Functioning to making a presentation or passing an exam. Many people feel anxious about presenting reports or taking tests. It can be nerve-wracking to speak in public or feel pressured to finish a test in time, knowing that you'll be evaluated on your performance. The good news is that the best remedy for presentation or test anxiety is simple preparation.

What's the best way to prepare for a presentation or exam? From Day 1 in a course, keep in mind that you will eventually need to discuss, summarize, or present just about everything you learn in that class. So active listening, reading, and note-taking throughout the entire course are the best preparation for whatever you'll be called upon to do. That way, preparing for an oral or written performance is the exact process *you're already doing* with every task.

YOU'VE ALREADY BEEN:
- Actively listening and taking notes
- Keeping up with reading
- And, most important, reviewing your notes regularly

DO AND REVIEW

Steps to prepare for a presentation or exam

"Sure," you might say. "I've been studying the material all along. But how do I actually prepare for a speech or an exam?" Keep the tips below in mind when preparing for any type of presentation, report, or test:

- Listen to the teacher and take good notes.

- Organize your information: Put your notes in order by date, keep handouts together, and know what material will be on the test or in your presentation.

- Review past notes to see if you still have questions on older material.

- Find out in advance what kind of exam or presentation it will be, since different strategies work best for different types of tests (such as essay, true/false, short-answer, math) or presentation (such as lecture, question-and-answer, slide show).

- Review what strategies have worked best for you.

- To plan your time, fill out your planner, starting with the date of the test or presentation and working backwards. Schedule what topics you will review, how long each review will take, and the dates and times you will review each.

- Write down and schedule the tasks for each step of your review. For example, will you be reading over your notes, creating a timeline, making flashcards with key vocabulary terms? Will you use bullet points to keep your speaking on track? Write out the entire presentation? Practice in front of the mirror or others?

- Save the night before the exam or presentation for reviewing, not learning new material. You can't learn all the material the night before, and it's wiser to save this night for a final review of what you have prepared so you go into the test or presentation feeling confident.

Guiding Questions for a presentation or exam

QUESTIONS TO ASK YOURSELF BEFORE A PRESENTATION OR EXAM	• Do I understand the purpose of the presentation and the directions? • Will I lose points for mistakes? • How much time do I have for each section?

STEPS TO FOLLOW DURING AN EXAM	• Before you write anything, read the directions carefully.
	• If possible, survey the entire exam to get the big picture before you begin.
	• Determine what kinds of questions you are being asked:
	  • Multiple Choice
	  • True/False
	  • Short Answer
	  • Essay
	  • Math
	• Budget your time for each section of the exam.
	• Slow down and calm yourself throughout the exam.
	• Review the exam thoroughly before you turn it in.

QUESTIONS TO ASK YOURSELF AFTER THE PRESENTATION OR EXAM	• Did I do as well as I thought I would? • What mistakes did I make? • Did I prepare the right material and use my preparation time effectively? • Is there anything I can improve on the next time?

DO AND REVIEW

Tips for specific types of performances or presentations

See the hints below to help you succeed with each kind of presentation or assessment. Steps to follow for multiple choice exams:

- Read the directions carefully.

- Read the questions first while covering up the answers. Try to answer the question first, and then look at the choices to see if your answer is there.

- If your answer is not there, eliminate the ones you know are wrong.

- Eliminate the answers that don't fit the question grammatically.

- If two or three options seem equally correct, "all of the above" may be the right answer.

- If two options seem to be direct opposites, chances are that one of those is correct.

- If two options seem correct, compare them for differences. Then go back to the question and find the better answer.

- Remember to look for the *best* answer, not just a correct one.

- Guess, unless there is a penalty for mistakes.

Steps to follow for true/false exams:

- Read the statement. Look for negatives such as *no, not*, or *cannot*, and look for double negatives.

- Reread the statement but drop the negative/s and see if what remains is true or false. Then, reinsert the negative/s to answer. For example, if a statement reads, "It cannot rain on a Sunday," drop the *not* to see if the sentence is true ("It can rain on a Sunday," which is true), and then reinsert *not* and judge the statement (false).

- Watch out for absolute words. Most things don't occur in absolutes. When the statement contains *no, never, none, always, every, entirely,* or *only* it increases the chances it will be incorrect, because it must be 100% true to be correct.

DO AND REVIEW

Steps to follow for short-answer exams:

- While preparing for a short-answer exam, focus on the main ideas rather than on details, so your answers include the most important points.

- Highlight your notes to make sure you understand the main idea of the topic you are learning.

- Practice expressing the main idea concisely with one or two supporting details. You may want to use a web to categorize each topic and add supporting details for each.

- While taking a short-answer exam, write your answers in concise but specific sentences. Pack in as much information as you can.

- Remember, a good or "educated" guess is better than leaving the item blank.

Steps to follow for essay exams:

- If visible to you, read through the entire exam before you start. Often essays come at the end of exams but are worth a lot of points. So, make sure to leave enough time to plan and complete the essay/s.

- If there is more than one essay question, read through them all before you start, and decide the order in which you will answer them. It may help to do the one demanding the most information first, so you'll have written down facts you may use in another essay.

- Pay attention to keywords in the question, such as *compare, contrast,* and *analyze*. These are your core directions.

- Plan before you write! Do a web or outline, making sure you have evidence for each of your points. Then, decide the order in which you will present your points (for example, most important to least important).

DO AND REVIEW

Creating a Web to Help with Essay Responses:

One way to organize your thoughts before writing a response to an essay question is to create a web with supporting ideas that branch out supporting details. In the example below, the writer has a clear main idea, three supporting ideas, and related details to each supporting idea.

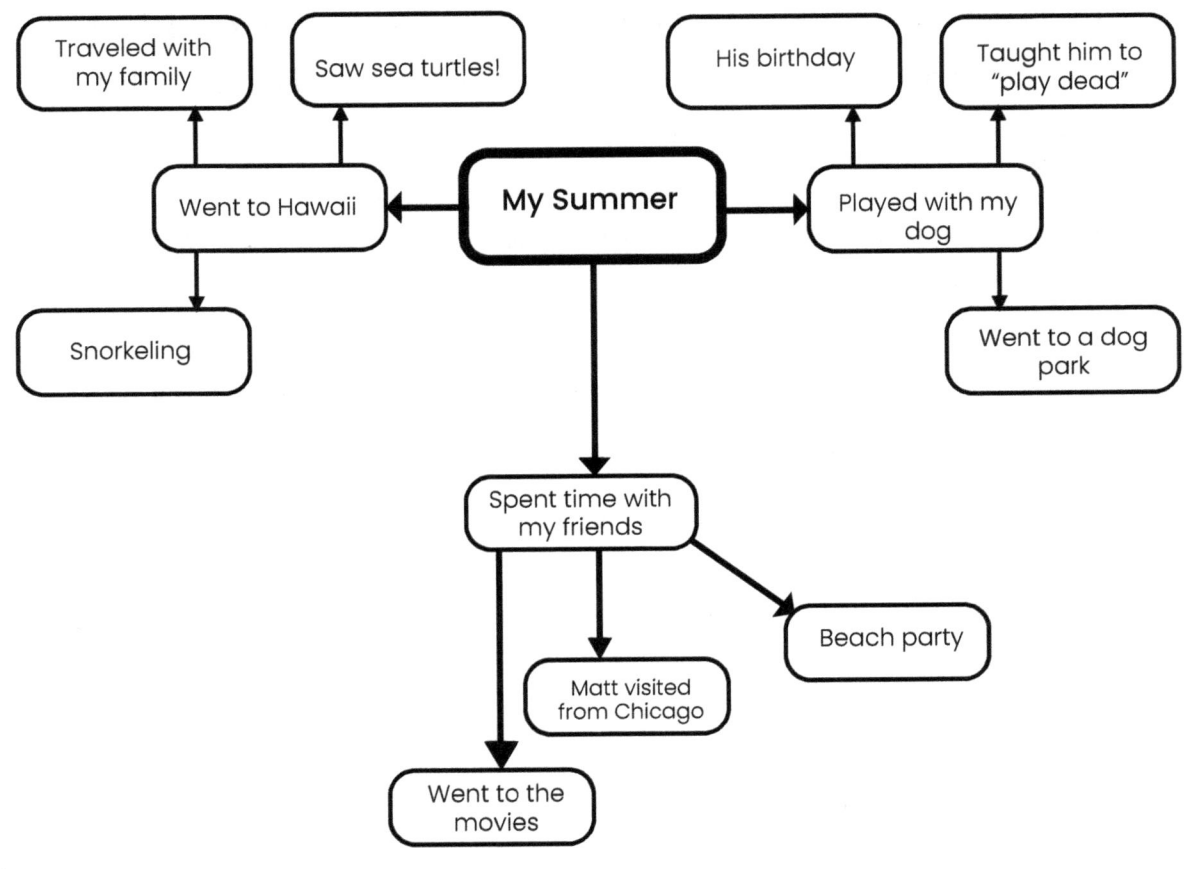

An outline for a 3-5 paragraph essay can be created from the web:

Paragraph 1: Introduction

- I had a great summer

Paragraph 2: Body Topic 1: Played with my dog

- His birthday
- Learned to "play dead"
- Went to a dog park

Paragraph 3: Body Topic 2: Spent time with my friends

- Went to the movies
- Matt visited from Chicago
- Beach party

Paragraph 4: Body Topic 3: Went to Hawaii

- Traveled with my family
- Snorkeling
- Saw sea turtles

Paragraph 5: Conclusion

- Sum up your points

DO AND REVIEW

The following map is an example of incomplete ideas. Note how the writer hasn't written details to support his ideas or made clear connections. For example, how is "Saw Matt" connected to "sea turtles"? The writer also has extra ideas about school, which don't seem connected to the main idea, "My summer".

When you have a good web of ideas, you can identify the best sub-topics and examples. You may generate more ideas than you need to include in your paper.

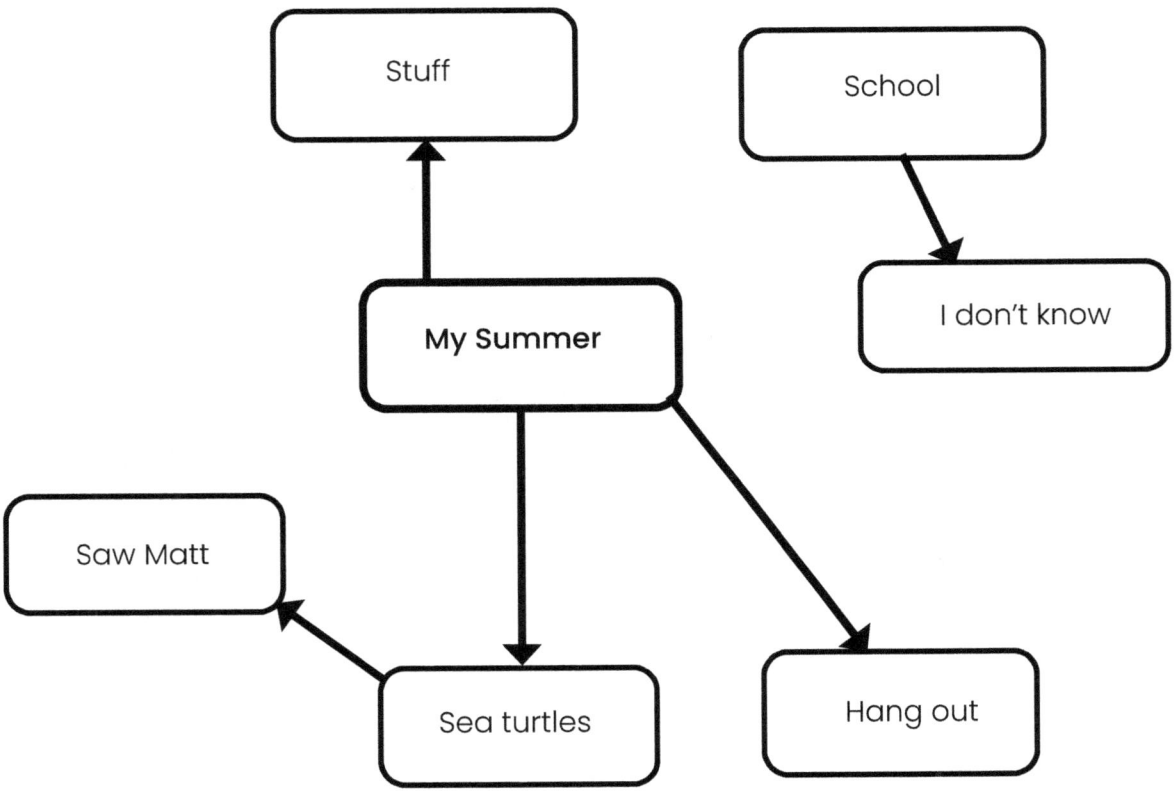

Once your ideas have been put in an outline you can begin writing a rough draft.

Follow good essay-writing rules:
- Begin with a clear thesis statement—the main point you're trying to prove.
- Support your thesis with good evidence.
- Summarize your points in the conclusion.
- Reread and edit your work.

Steps to follow for math exams:

PREPARING for math exams:
- Take good notes in class.
- Do all your homework and make sure you understand the problems. If you don't understand the problems, write down a question to ask your teacher.
- Meet with your teacher to clarify the concepts.
- Take practice exams and do chapter review problems to get used to doing problems in different formats and in the amount of time you will have for the exam.

DURING math exams:
- Read the directions.
- Talk yourself through each problem.
- Show every step of your work clearly.
- Double-check your work along the way.
- Make sure you're following the correct sign.
- If you get stuck, go to another problem, and return to the hard problem later.

DO AND REVIEW

Apps to avoid distractions:

These are some of the apps that offer different programs helping with avoiding distractions. Check them out with a teacher, parent, or coach.

Note: New programs are constantly being created, so once you determine the features you're looking for, you can search for a program that best answers your needs.

Apps to Help You Stay Focused		
App	Description	Where
Self-Control	Blocks all other apps and websites for a set time and it's impossible to undo.	Free, on Mac OS only
StayFocused	A Google Chrome extension that restricts the time you can spend on too-engaging websites, with some allotted time planned.	Free, on all devices
Freedom	App and website blocker that can be scheduled and plays optional ambient background noise.	$6.99/ month, on all devices
Cold Turkey Blocker	Block only specific websites and apps or the entire internet, with listed exceptions.	$39, one time purpose for life, on all devices

DO AND REVIEW

UNIT FIVE

CHECK AND TURN IN

Did I Meet My Goal?

Checking to make sure you met your goal for each task you complete is the last step of your Executive Functioning plan. You've already learned and have been applying the STOP AND IMAGINE, THINK AND PLAN, DO AND REVIEW guidelines. This unit, CHECK AND TURN IN, is the final step for success!

EXECUTIVE FUNCTIONING SKILLS TO HELP YOU CHECK AND TURN IN YOUR WORK:

> **CHECK AND TURN IN**
> Executive Functioning Skills

SHIFTING	Moving from one idea or activity to another
MONITORING	Judging the quality and pace of work
INHIBITION	Stopping off-task behavior
EMOTIONAL CONTROL	Regulating stress and distractibility

You have worked hard to identify your goal, break it down into manageable parts, and do each step. If you skip the final CHECK, you might miss the crucial step necessary to ensure that what you have done matches what you set out to do.

It's best to check your work along the way. When you check an item off your checklist, make sure it matches your expectations and the task that was assigned. When you complete the full task, check again that each step was completed correctly.

CHECK AND TURN IN

Monitoring is the most important Executive Functioning skill for checking your work, but it calls on other skills, too. To monitor your work, you must inhibit your desire to turn it in without checking. Shift your mind about the assignment if you find an error and look for a better way to express your ideas. Your Working Memory is needed to make sure you remember all the directions for the assignment, and emotional control is needed to ensure that you stay calm and allot yourself the time to monitor that the work you did matches the assignment and your own goals for it.

Executive Functioning Skills to help you Check and Turn In work

Monitoring: Judging the quality and pace of your work

A person with a weak ability to monitor often:
- Is the first to turn in work and the most shocked by its poor reception
- Is convinced she or he is thoroughly prepared and finds the test or assignment much more difficult than expected
- Makes very basic errors in math problems or writing
- Has poor "audience awareness," speaking too slowly or quickly or at too low or high a level, and missing social cues from the audience
- Yawns, slumps their shoulders, rub their eyes, but denies being tired when someone asks

Using the checklists you created in Unit 3, THINK AND PLAN, will get you in the habit of checking on your progress as you work. The trick is to become aware of the areas that challenge you so you can focus your attention on them.

Exercise: Self-Monitoring

No Materials Needed

Instructions

Give the prompt: *"Let's imagine that there's a monitoring device 30 feet above you, and it's carefully and helpfully watching you work."*

Imagine it: *"What does it look like?"*

Own it: *"What does it notice about your work?" Does it see anything missing from your work?"* If the student says something's missing from her/ his work, ask *"Who can you find to check it with you?"*

Extend it: *"How can you use this monitor to help you complete your work?"*

CHECK AND TURN IN

Shifting: Moving from one idea or activity to another

The importance of the ability to shift was discussed in Unit 2 and Unit 3. Shifting, or making changes as you plan and work, lets you correct errors you made or add in anything you left out. It's the talent of staying open to good changes.

When you check your work, you need to consider what the person who will receive the work expects. Try to shift your mindset from your own to that of the audience or grader.

Checklist: Is My Work Complete?

Worker →	Reviewer
Have I met my deadline?	Was this turned in on time?
Does my work match what I was assigned?	Does this work match the task?
Did I follow all the steps?	Are all the details correct in this task?
What feedback do I need to make sure this is my best work?	What feedback would be the most clear and helpful?

Inhibition: The ability to stop off task actions when you need to.

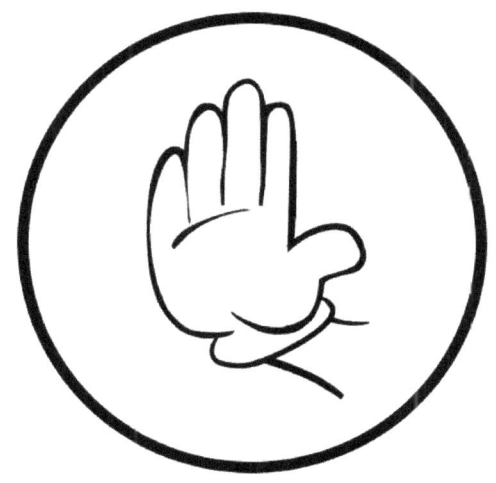

As you learned in Unit 2, inhibition is the power to stop off-task actions when you need to. For example, checking your work requires the ability to inhibit your desire to be done with your work NOW—even though you know making sure you checked off each step on your plan significantly increase your chances of meeting your goals. Practicing the skill of inhibition will strengthen your new habit of overcoming this challenge so you can set off-task actions aside while you still need to work.

CHECK AND TURN IN

Emotional Control: Regulating stress and distractibility

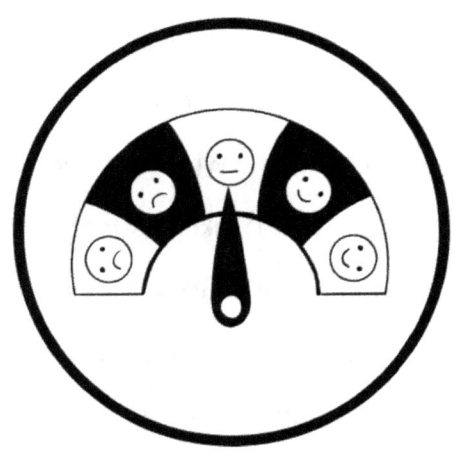

The related skill of Emotional Control has popped up throughout this workbook, since responding inappropriately to a situation can throw off your best intentions. Even when the emotion is positive—the joyful sense of freedom after you completed a task—letting that feeling rule your behavior may keep you from finishing other crucial steps in your TO DO list, such as checking your work and turning it in. Having Emotional Control means you can save your well-deserved celebration until you've done the checking and making any needed changes.

Staying with a Task all the way to Completion

Completing work can be difficult due to pacing or time management difficulties. A good understanding of beginning, middle, and ending is important for students to understand so they can monitor how far they are in a task. To get to the end of task students need emotional control and flexible thinking to get past any frustrations that make them want to stop before they are 100% completed with their work.

Focuser or Distractor? Who's in control?

Students can use their creativity to get an idea of what it's like to be able to control their actions. We all have a part of ourselves that can stay focused no matter what happens. If a child is in class and someone drops a pencil, or they realize they forgot their lunch while they're taking a test, the focused child can inhibit their behavior and stay engaged in what they are doing. The focused student can tell themselves to finish the test and then they'll deal with what they need to later.

We also all have a distracted part us. This is the part of all of us that takes us off task, so when a student hears a pencil drop or realizes they forgot their lunch they stop focusing on what they are doing and instead pay attention to the pencil or lunch. The Distractor takes us completely off task so that we're not able to finish what's in front of us.

This exercise has students imagine being the Focuser and the Distractor in different situations. Students can become aware of what it looks like and feels like when they're distracted or when they're focused. The goal is to help students identify with their Focuser and learn to engage it when they need it.

CHECK AND TURN IN

Exercise: Who's in Charge?

Materials

Drawing materials, clay, puppets, or cards. You can also use online resources:

- onlinepuppets.org
- onlinesandtray.com
- oaklandertraining.org/projective-cards

Instructions

Give the prompt: *"Let's imagine that you have a part of you called The Focuser, who is really good at staying on task; and you have a part of you called The Distractor, who has a hard time staying focused due to all the interesting things going on around them."*

Step 1

- **Imagine it FOCUSED:** *"Imagine what it feels like when you're fully focused on an activity.*

- **Make it:** *"Draw a picture, or pick an object, card or puppet that reminds you of that feeling."* Give the student a few minutes to draw or to pick an item.

Step 2

- **Imagine it DISTRACTED:** *"Now, imagine what it feels like when you can't stay focused on an activity— when your mind keeps getting distracted thinking of other things you need or want to do".*

- **Make it:** *"Draw a picture, or pick an object, card or puppet that reminds you of that feeling."* Give the student a few minutes to draw or to pick an item.

Step 3

- **Be it:** *"OK, let's imagine a likely scenario. Let's imagine you reading a book in class and how your Focuser and your Distractor act. Use your Focuser [drawing / card / puppet] to show how it feels reading in a focused way. Now, use your Distractor [drawing / card / puppet] to show how it feels reading in a distracted way."*

- **Own it:** *"What advice would your Focuser give your Distractor to help decrease the distractions? Let's imagine how your Focuser and your Distractor act when you're doing your homework and it's taking a long time. Use your Focuser [drawing / card / puppet] to show how it feels to do your homework efficiently. "*

- **Extend it:** *"Now, use your Distractor [drawing / card / puppet] to show how it feels to do your homework inefficiently. What advice would your Focuser give your Distractor to help decrease the distractions?"* Finally, ask the student, *"What other situations in your life involve your Focuser and your Distractor? What advice would your Focuser give your Distractor to help you sharpen your attention in those situations?"*

Exercise: Beginning, Middle, End

Materials

Drawing materials, clay, puppets, or cards. You can also use online resources:

- onlinepuppets.org
- onlinesandtray.com
- oaklandertraining.org/projective-cards

Instructions

Give the prompt: *"Completing tasks can be challenging. But remembering there's a beginning, middle, and end to each task lets you monitor your progress from start to finish. Knowing if you're at the beginning, middle or end of a task helps you overcome any obstacles keeping you from completing it.*

Beginning	Middle	End
• **Imagine it:** *"Imagine what it feels like when you're just starting a project—the beginning."*	• **Imagine it:** *"Imagine what it feels like when you're right in the middle of a project—when you've done a lot of work but still have more to do."*	• **Imagine it:** *"Imagine what it feels like when you've finished a project all the way to the end."*

Beginning	Middle	End
• **Make it:** *"Draw a picture or pick an object, card or puppet that reminds you of that feeling."* Give the student a few moments to draw or to pick an object.	• **Make it:** *"Draw a picture or pick an object, card or puppet that reminds you of that feeling."* Give the student a few moments to draw or to pick an object.	• **Make it:** *"Draw a picture or pick an object, card or puppet that reminds you of that feeling."* Give the student a few moments to draw or to pick an object.

Own it: Ask the student: *"Think of a current homework assignment you have. Now, imagine you've been working on it for 5 minutes."* Leave a moment for the student to respond, then ask:

- *"How do you feel? Does that feeling match the feeling you described when you're at the beginning, middle or end of a task? So, what stage is your homework assignment in— beginning, middle or end? Is there a next step to complete it?"*

Extend it: Tell the student, *"Let's pick another situation. Imagine a long-term assignment you have to do."*

- *Now, imagine you've been working on it for 2 days."* Leaving a moment for the student to respond, ask: *"How do you feel? Does that feeling match the feeling you described when you're at the beginning, middle or end?"*

CHECK AND TURN IN

Using your CHECK AND TURN In skills

Checklist: Guiding Questions to Check Your Work

You have learned all the steps to complete your work. Now, you need to take a moment to review your work and make sure you achieved your goal. Use the checklist below to review your work.

QUESTIONS	ANSWERS
Did I complete each step of the plan?	
I am happy with the work I did on each step?	
Does the final product match my expectations?	
Does the final product match the guidelines for the task?	
Is the final product better or worse than I expected?	
Is there something I would have done differently if I did this again?	
Is anything missing?	

©2023 KandMCenter.com

Checklist: Turn it in

Don't forget the final step of turning your work in. Where is the best place for you to store the work? If you are turning it in in class, place the paper in your backpack in a special homework section so you can easily find it. If you are turning it in online, take the time to login and send it when you are done.

Check Your Work

STOP	THINK	DO	CHECK
• Did I complete everything assigned?	• What was I supposed to do? • Did I do it all? Am I happy with my work? • Will the teacher be happy with my work? • Is it ready to turn in?	• Turn it into the teacher in class or online.	• Did the teacher get it?

UNIT SIX
REASSESS

REASSESS

Now that you've completed the Executive Functioning Workbook, how do you feel about your skills? Are there areas you feel more confident about than before? Are there areas you want to keep developing? Take a moment to review the skills and to think about what you have learned.

Executive Functioning skills to review:

Executive Functioning Component

REVIEW Executive functioning Skills	
INITIATION	Starting work
SHIFT	Moving from one idea or activity to another
INHIBITION	Stopping off-task behavior
WORKING MEMORY	Remembering information for immediate use
PLANNING	Setting goals and the steps to accomplish them
ORGANIZING MATERIALS	Tracking items in workspaces
TIME MANAGEMENT	Allotting appropriate time for each task
MONITORING	Judging the quality and pace of work
EMOTIONAL CONTROL	Regulating stress and distractibility

REASSESS

Time to Reflect

Take a moment to think over the work you've done during this program. Did you meet your goals? Are you on your way to achieving your goals?

Exercise: Rate Your Skills

You worked hard learning about Executive Functioning and practicing skills. At the beginning of this program, you took a quiz to discover your Executive Functioning strengths and weaknesses. Now that you've completed the course, how would you rate yourself?

1 - Weak 5- Strong	Rating
Working Memory Remembering information for immediate use	
Organizing Materials Tracking items in workspaces	
Planning Tasks Setting goals and the steps to accomplish them	
Emotional Control Regulating stress and distractibility	
Initiating Work Starting work	
Inhibiting Behavior Stopping off-task behavior	
Monitoring Judging the quality and pace of work	
Shift Moving from one idea or activity to another	
Time Management Allotting appropriate time for each task	

REASSESS

Exercise: Reflect On What Worked For You

Ask yourself these questions as you move beyond this course:

- What was the most helpful thing I learned?
- What practices do I want to continue?
- How can I continue to set myself up for success?
- What areas should I remind myself to focus on?
- Am I using my calendar and planner effectively?
- Am I keeping my workspace clear?
- Do I continue to keep my workspace stocked with the supplies I need?
- Am I using my time wisely?
- Am I willing to do the work to continue building my Executive Functioning skills?

Plan for the future

"Practice makes perfect" in most activities, including Executive Functioning skills, which grow more powerful by continued focus and exercise. Research shows that it's never too late to learn new skills—really, to lay down new neuropathways. And because the brain processes information best through well-used paths, the pathways that are frequently used get stronger and faster. That's why reviewing learned information and practicing learned behaviors lets you retrieve and deploy them more quickly.

Use the support until you master the skills

This program provided you with the support you needed to establish and use new Executive Functioning skills. Learning new skills is like building a high-rise building:

- First, you build the scaffolding outside the building to support the framework on the inside.
- Then you practice the skills until they become comfortable and easy.
- Once the foundation is strong, the scaffolding can be taken down.

This workbook, with its checklists, charts, study plans, apps, and check-ins, was the scaffolding that supported your Executive Functioning development. Now that you have integrated the skills and made them habitual, you no longer need all the external support. You may choose to keep using the ones you like but know that you are now an independent learner. That knowledge, and the talent you've polished of setting your goals and guiding yourself to achieve them, are great and rewarding accomplishments.

APPENDIX

APPENDIX

Example apps, extensions, and websites mentioned:

Calendar and planner apps:

App	Description	Where
Microsoft To Do	Daily planner, task manager, reminders, attachments, sharing, and more.	Free on all devices
Google Calendar	Allows for sync option for events and schedules from a Google account with other apps, events, and schedules.	Free on all devices
Google Tasks	Set due dates and reminders. Can create multiple lists for different Google accounts and add emails to tasks for collaboration.	Free on all devices
Trello	Collaborative app for meetings, projects, events, and goal setting.	Free, with paid upgrades available, on all devices
My Study Life-School Planner	Track tasks, store assignments and exams in the cloud, accessible anywhere. Manage classes with timetables and notifications.	Free on all devices
Todoist	Manage and share tasks, subtasks, sub-projects, recurring tasks, notifications, different priorities, and more.	Free, with paid upgrades available, on all devices

APPENDIX

App	Description	Where
TimeTimer	Turns phone, computer, or smartwatch screen into a fun, bold, circle timer.	Free on all devices

Apps to avoid distractions:

App	Description	Where
Self-Control	Blocks all other apps and websites for a set time and it's impossible to undo.	Free, on Mac OS only
StayFocused	A Google Chrome extension that restricts the time you can spend on too-engaging websites, with some allotted time planned.	Free on all devices
Freedom	App and website blocker that can be scheduled and plays optional ambient background noise.	$6.99/month, on all devices
Cold Turkey Blocker	Block only specific websites and apps or the entire internet, with listed exceptions.	$39, one time purpose for life, on all devices

Note-taking apps:

App	Description	Where
Notability	Mark up imported documents, record/playback audio, create schedules, sync to Dropbox or Google Drive.	Free on all devices, with some in-app purchases
Notation	Notes app, a task and project manager, and a reference wiki with easy collaboration capabilities.	Free on all devices, for personal users. $10/month/user for team functions.
ScanMarker	Scan physical texts into a digital document. It can also translate and read aloud text.	Software free, on all devices. Marker is $109
Temi	Speech-to-text app. Upload any audio or video file, then download the transcript.	$0.25/minute
GoodNotes	Digital notebook for document organization and editing. It can import, sync, draw, and erase.	$7.99, one-time purchase. Mac iOS only

www.ingramcontent.com/pod-product-compliance
Lightning Source LLC
Chambersburg PA
CBHW080518030426
42337CB00023B/4558